CHINA SPEAKS

On the Conflict Between China and Japan

CHINA SPEAKS

On the Conflict Between China and Japan

By

CHIH MENG

With an Introduction by

His Excellency W. W. YEN,

KENNIKAT PRESS
Port Washington, N. Y./London

CHINA SPEAKS

First published in 1932
Reissued in 1970 by Kennikat Press
Library of Congress Catalog Card No: 74-115205
ISBN 0-8046-1098-3

Manufactured by Taylor Publishing Company   Dallas, Texas

INTRODUCTION

By His Excellency W. W. YEN

Chief Delegate of China to the League of Nations
Minister of China to the United States

FOR years past, the Japanese publicists have taken great pains to convince the world that the control or possession of Manchuria is vital to the existence of Japan. They have appealed on sentimental or historical grounds; they have elaborated its economic necessity; and they have argued on grounds of military necessity.

The greatest difficulty with these Japanese spokesmen is that they think only of the national existence and defense of Japan, while it never seems to occur to them that China has her needs too. What about the national existence of China, the national defense of China, the economic requirements of China, and the strategic necessity of Manchuria to China?

Historically and sentimentally, Manchuria has been part of China for centuries and it is the home of millions of Chinese. That Japan fought Russia on Chinese soil and that a large number of Japanese soldiers lost their lives in Manchuria, constitutes no valid reason for the preposterous claims which have been constantly put forward by the Japanese spokesmen.

▼

34432

Economically, Manchuria is destined to play a very important role in the industrial development of China. Manchuria contains some of the best coal fields. China is not at all well supplied with iron and Manchuria has the largest iron deposit. With its growing population, China has to import annually large amounts of food stuffs; Manchuria with its rich soil is looked upon as the granary for China's millions. China, no less than Japan, is faced with the problem of surplus population, especially in the provinces along the coast. Exclusion laws operate against Chinese emigrants even harder than they do against Japanese. Hence, enormous numbers of immigrants have yearly poured into the Three Eastern Provinces during the last decade. These are elemental economic problems that are facing the Chinese people, which no thinking people can ignore.

Strategically, Manchuria is absolutely vital to China's security. Chinese history has taught that China's security depends upon an adequate defense of its northern boundary. During the last thousand years, China has witnessed two invasions, each of which led to a domination of China for several hundred years. Both of them came from beyond the Great Wall. The fact is that whoever holds South Manchuria is the master of North China. Strategically, South Manchuria commands a dominating position over the great plains of Central Asia, and it is well-nigh impossible to defend these plains against powerful attacks from the northeast. If Manchuria is spoken of as the first line of defense of Japan, what about China? Where is China's first line of defense and where is China's second line of defense?

The Chinese are not so unreasonable as to ignore the

reasonable and legitimate needs and aspirations of the Japanese people. Japan is our nearest neighbour, and we sincerely desire to be at peace with our neighbours. For many centuries the Japanese people have shared the heritage of our civilization. As it has been admitted by one of the leading Japanese savants, "Your civilization (Chinese) has been our (Japanese) civilization, your history has been our history, your language has been our language, your art and philosophy has been our art and philosophy." We are happy to see the phenomenal rise of modern Japan and her rapid progress and great prosperity. But, when she blindly pursues her own interests in utter disregard of China's vital interests, and when she is bent on imperialistic conquest without any consideration for China's needs and aspirations, China must resist for her self-respect and self-preservation.

On the night of September 18, 1931, Japan startled the world by suddenly launching her great war machine against China. There was no warning; there were no diplomatic preliminaries; no attempts to discuss alleged grievances or to negotiate. Since then, the sky of the Far East has been red with the glare of burning cities and villages; and the tramp of Japan's armies and the thunder of her guns have been heard throughout Manchuria, at Shanghai, at Nanking and elsewhere in China. More than two thousand square miles of Chinese territory and thirty millions of Chinese people are today under the Japanese yoke. What is it all about? This book is intended to answer that question. Various pretexts and excuses for an aggression which has few historic parallels have been put forward by Japan. They are here dealt with as dispassionately and objectively as possible in order that public opinion may understand and judge them. I venture to bespeak an attentive consideration not only of the fundamental merits of the dispute but of the principles which underlie it and extend far beyond the immediate interests of the two parties.

That the World War profoundly stirred the conscience of civilized men is a truism. That men's subsequent efforts to profit by the lesson and improve their condition are really bearing fruit, is not yet so clear as to carry conviction. The ambitious attempt to organize peace on a permanent basis has commanded universal sympathy and given unbounded hope. The founding of the League of Nations has been properly recognized as an event of the first importance. The movement for disarmament has been another encouraging factor. The notable increase in the number of arbitration treaties is significant. Finally, the simple and impressive renunciation of war, solemnly recorded in the Kellogg-Briand Pact, has been welcomed with a sympathetic understanding by people of every race and condition.

All of these things together make up what we may call the NEW ORDER in the affairs of nations. Will this NEW ORDER gather to itself strength and survive; or is it destined to find disaster on the rocks of human selfishness, greed, and materialism?

The Sino-Japanese controversy is the first great test. The OLD ORDER is here pitted against the New. Japan, though a participant in all of the measures taken to build up the modern system of right, has chosen the ancient method of might to settle her dispute with China. Japan's appeal to arms is a direct challenge to the NEW ORDER. China,

on the other hand, rests her cause squarely on the founda-
tions which have been so carefully laid for the peaceful adjustment of all international differences. She has kept the
Covenant of the League and now invokes its protection. She
asks that the Nine Power Treaty, which was made at the
first Disarmament Conference specifically to guarantee her
full opportunity to work out her own problems in peace, be
observed. She offers to submit the whole dispute to arbitration or judicial settlement as the Covenant and the Kellogg-Briand Pact require.

I commend this book as one of far more than casual
interest. It deals with a problem of vital concern to every
member of a society which is trying to organize itself for
development in peace and security.

W. W. YEN.

GENEVA,
    March 10, 1932.

INTRODUCTION

By W. W. WILLOUGHBY

Professor of Political Science, Johns Hopkins University

I HAVE adopted with pleasure the suggestion of the author of this volume that I should write a few words of introduction, since it gives to me the opportunity of stressing certain points which, it seems to me, deserve emphasis.

During the long period which has ensued since she first came into open conflict with China, Japan, though professing friendliness to her neighbor, has done nothing in an affirmative way to aid China in building up for herself a strong, united, and economically prosperous national existence. Upon the contrary, she has seized what have seemed to her to be favorable opportunities .to impair China's sovereignty and to break down her administrative integrity. Even as to the conceding to China of the right, enjoyed by other sovereign nations, to derive an adequate income from her customs receipts, Japan was among the last of the foreign Powers to yield, and then under not unimportant conditions.

Especially with regard to Manchuria, Japan, for a generation, has exhibited, in the clearest manner, a determination to extend not only her economic interests but her political control. In this connection it is significant to observe that, at the Washington Conference, although prevailed upon by the pressure of the other Powers, and especially of

the United States, to cease from exercising in China certain
forms of interference with China's sovereignty, Japan made
practically no specific concessions as regards Manchuria.
She did, indeed, concede that Manchuria was an integral
part of China, and did agree "to respect the sovereignty, the
independence, and the territorial and administrative integrity" of China, but it is clear that she did not abandon her
desire and intention to bring Manchuria under her substan-
tive, if not formal or technical, political control. Japan's
recent acts have, therefore, a deeper significance than, perhaps, they would otherwise appear to have.

Manchuria, during recent years, has greatly increased its
population and its foreign trade, but there is no convincing
evidence that this has been due to philanthropic efforts upon
the part of Japan. The South Manchuria Railway has, indeed, played an important part in the economic development of the country, but Japan did not build this railway,
but obtained it as a spoil of war, and it cannot be proved that
the railway would not have been a powerful economic instrument in the hands of the Chinese. Certainly, whatever
may have been the advantages which Manchuria has derived from a Japanese operation of the South Manchuria
Railway, it is a fact that Japan has exerted a powerful, and,
in a number of cases successful, influence in the preventing
of other needed railways in Manchuria.

Japan has complained of inadequate security for her nationals and their property in China. It is, however, to be
observed that many more Chinese living in Japan and Jap-
anese-governed Korea have lost their lives through lawless
violence than have Japanese living in China. And, in this

connection, there is to be noted the remarkable immunity from personal violence of Japanese nationals living in other parts of China following the Japanese invasion of Manchuria in September last. As is well known, and as was but natural, this invasion created a high degree of indignation upon the part of the Chinese throughout China. This indignation might have been expected to lead to attacks by Chinese upon Japanese living in China and far distant from any protecting Japanese military forces, but, in obedience to an exhortation from their Government, the Chinese, in this respect, exhibited a remarkable degree of self control. This obedience, under such provocative circumstances, bears an eloquent testimony to the moral authority possessed by those in political authority in China over those whom they rule.

Mr. Meng, the author of this volume, has set forth in a clear manner the nature of the controversy submited by China to the League of Nations, and yet there is, perhaps, one point with regard to that controversy which, it seems to the writer, needs rather more emphasis. This point is that a clear line of distinction needs to be drawn between the question as to the propriety of the acts of Japan since the outbreak of September last, as tested by the requirements of the Covenant of the League, and the merits of the various controversies which lie back of and antedate the outbreak of September 18th. Whatever may have been the validity of the claims of Japan that China has been at fault in various respects in her dealings with Japan, or with her nationals, the controversy with which the League has had as yet to deal, has been with regard to the propriety and legality of Japanese acts in attempting to correct her conceived grievances. Only when the situation created by these acts has been effectively dealt with will the League be called upon to correct, if asked by the parties so to do, the underlying causes of controversy between China and Japan. China has agreed that, when this time comes, she is prepared and willing to have these issues submitted either to arbitration, to judicial determination at the hands of the Permanent Court of Justice, or, if neither of these means is acceptable to Japan, to inquiry and judgment by the Council of the League as provided for in the Covenant of the League.

The distinction which has just been discussed has been kept steadily in mind by those who have conducted China's case before the League, but the writer is not sure that the general public for whom this volume has been prepared, has been sufficiently aware of it.

Although neither the Council nor the Assembly of the League has declared, in a direct manner that, from the beginning of the outbreak in September, Japan has been acting in violation of her obligations as a Member of the League, both of these League organs have shown, by necessary implication, that such is their opinion. Indeed, several of the representatives of the members of the League have not hesitated individually so to declare, and there has not been a single one of them who has ventured to assert affirmatively that Japan has been acting within her rights.

As to China's and Japan's conduct since the submission of the controversy to the League, the following public statement by one who for years has been a foremost advocate of peace and supporter of the League, deserves quotation. Lord Robert Cecil, in the course of a long and formal address to the General Council of the League of Nations Union, at an emergency meeting held February 27, 1932, in London, said,

One other fact I am bound to call your attention to. Whatever may be the rights of the matter as between Japan and China—I am talking of the ultimate controversy between them—as far as the relations of those two powers to the League of Nations are concerned there can be no question. China has throughout acted in accordance with what she believed to be the wishes of the League. She has refrained more than once from taking strong action at the behest of the League. She has professed from the outset her readiness to place her whole case in the hands of the League and to accept whatever decision the League may give. Now I would not have said as much as this except that respect for Viscount Ishii [the reference here is to a letter to the London *Times* signed by Viscount Ishii and other distinguished men] compels me to explain what is the thought, not of myself, which matters very little indeed, but of thousands, and, indeed, I believe of hundreds of thousands of my fellow countrymen throughout the world, and of the nationals of countries in different parts of the world, in reference to this dispute. We cannot evade the conclusion that throughout this matter China has acted as a loyal and honourable member of the League of Nations and many of us feel that it would be a very grave exaggeration to say the same of Japan.

Before closing these few words of introduction the writer cannot refrain from expressing his admiration of the manner in which China's representatives have conducted her case before the Council and the Assembly of the League. Until the close of the Council's session in December, China's representative was Dr. S. K. Alfred Sze. Physically exhausted by his three months of continuous, strenuous labor, he was obliged to yield the chief direction to Dr. W. W. Yen, who, since then, and in an equally brilliant manner, has carried on the contest for justice and right.

W. W. WILLOUGHBY.

BALTIMORE,
    March 28, 1932.

FOREWORD

Lincoln is reported to have said, "You can fool some of the people all the time; all the people some of the time; but not all the people all the time." This was Lincoln's ingenious way of saying honesty is the best policy. Unfortunately, some publicists have no use for this truth, and, during an international crisis, they are the first ones to make out "perfect" cases for their respective countries.

During the present crisis the United States and the League of Nations have written a new chapter in diplomatic history. In the notes of Secretary of State Stimson and the Council and Assembly meetings of the League of Nations even diplomats have called a spade a spade. May not individuals, even patriots, discard the attitude of "my country, be it right or wrong, my country," and get down to fundamental issues.

The inertia of the old is great and the path of new habit-forming is difficult. It requires the highest order of individual and group discipline. The Chinese people, even in their intense suffering and distress, want civilization to advance and not to retreat.

It is the privilege of the author to take this opportunity to express the deep appreciation of the Chinese people to Professor W. W. Willoughby of Johns Hopkins University for his devotion to the cause of China for many years, and especially during the critical months immediately following China's appeal to the League of Nations last September when he was adviser to the Chinese Delegation to the League. The author is personally greatly indebted to Professor Willoughby and also to Mr. Grover Clark, former editor and publisher of the *Peking Leader* and now Consultant on Far Eastern Affairs in New York, for their kindness in making valuable criticism and in reading the manuscript.

CHIH MENG.

NEW YORK,
  March 31, 1932.

CONTENTS

CONTENTS

APPENDICES

PART ONE

THE CONFLICT

CHAPTER I

MANCHURIA

MANCHURIA has been characterized as "the cockpit of Asia" and "the cradle of conflict." The fault is certainly not with the land or with the people. Unlike the Balkans or Alsace-Lorraine, Manchuria has not changed sovereignty and boundaries for centuries. The population is highly homogeneous; there has never been any race-problem. In fact, Manchuria has a higher content of 100 per cent Chinese than America has of 100 per cent Americans.

In location, it is the northeastern corner of China just as New England is the northeastern corner of the United States.

The whole territory is located in the temperate zone between 38°47′ to 53° north latitude. Its area is about 384,000 square miles—more than three times the combined area of New England and New York states. Its important harbor, Dairen, is on the same latitude as San Francisco, St. Louis, Lisbon and Constantinople. Harbin, the most important commercial center in North Manchuria, is on the same latitude as Portland (Oregon), St. Paul (Minnesota), Ottawa (Canada), Milan, the south of Paris, and Vienna. The southern part is very old. It was a province of China called Liaotung during the Chou dynasty (1122-224 B.C.). The northern part is more like the great western states of Amer-

3

ica. Only the Chinese "covered wagon" movement has been going on over land and sea and in much larger numbers.

The northern part of Manchuria became an integral part of China in the Ching dynasty (A.D. 1644-1911). The home of the Manchu people was in northern Manchuria. When they occupied southern Manchuria and established the Ching dynasty, the whole of Manchuria came under the rule of one central government one hundred and thirty-two years before the American Revolution. Thus the name of Manchou, or Manchuria, came into use.

The historical claim of China to sovereignty over Manchuria has been undisputed for nearly three hundred years, since the Manchu dynasty established itself on the throne of China in 1644. Within recent years, Chinese sovereignty in Manchuria has been explicitly recognized by the great powers. In reply to a question in the House of Commons on July 13, 1928, Sir Austen Chamberlain declared that Great Britain considered Manchuria a part of China and recognized no special Japanese interests in it except those specially conferred by treaty and outlined by Baron Shidehara at the Washington Conference. On May 21, 1928, the American Secretary of State, Mr. Frank B. Kellogg, stated to the press, "As far as the United States is concerned, Manchuria is essentially Chinese soil." (T. A. Bisson in *"Basic Treaty Issues in Manchuria Between China and Japan,"* Foreign Policy Reports, December 23, 1931.)

Therefore, Manchuria is part of China because of priority in political affiliation and by explicit international recognition.

The Chinese people have been colonizing Manchuria peacefully for centuries. For a short period of time in the Ching dynasty the Government attempted to stop migration into Manchuria from other parts of China and to reserve the land for the Manchus, but that law was never effectively nor strictly enforced. Since the establishment of the Ching dynasty, the Manchus, or Manchurians, have either moved inside the Great Wall or intermarried with the Chinese.

The Manchus in Manchuria today are somewhat in the position of Indians in the United States, except that the Manchus have been entirely assimilated into Chinese culture. The few Manchu remnants have long abandoned the Manchurian language. The Chinese and Manchus now speak one dialect. In language, customs, traditions, and sentiments, Manchuria and China are one. In the social and political thinking of the Chinese people today, there is absolutely no distinction between a Manchu and a Chinese. In adopting the Chinese culture and through inter-marriage, the Manchus have united voluntarily with the Chinese race. Today, about 97 per cent of the people in Manchuria are Chinese.

The population in Manchuria, according to the latest estimate by Grover Clark for the end of 1930 in "Manchuria: A Survey of Its Economic Development," is as follows:

Approximate No. of		Per Cent of Total
Japanese	220,000	.7
Koreans or Chosenese	562,000	2.3
Chinese	30,000,000	96.5

Therefore, Manchuria is an integral part of China because of political unity, majority population, and cultural identity.

Nature's Favorite

Like the state of Pennsylvania, Manchuria is abundantly blessed by nature, excepting that the latter is eight times the size of the former. Rich mines and forests are added to fertile plains. The climate is favorable to agriculture, and the navigable rivers and ice-free harbors facilitate trade. Long before Japan appeared on the scene, Manchuria had already become prosperous. Sir Alexander Hosie, twice British Consul General in Manchuria and an authority on China, wrote in 1901 in his book—"Manchuria, Its People, Resources, and Recent History"—

I have travelled in different parts of China, I have seen great salt and piece goods traffic between Ssu-Ch'uan, Kwei-chow and Yunnan, but I never saw a sight which from its magnitude impressed me so much with the vast trade of China as the carrying trade from North to South in Manchuria.

Kuan-cheng-tzu, which lies on the left bank of Yi-tung, a tributary of the Sungari, is, as stated above, the chief commercial mart in Manchuria. It is the distributing centre for trade to and from Northern Kirin, Hei-lung-chiang and Eastern Mongolia. The city itself, the population of which is estimated at about 120,000. . . . Besides being a distributing centre, it is also the seat of several important industries, such as the manufacture of indigo and felt.

In spring, summer and autumn, a forest of masts lines the north bank of the Liao opposite the town of Newchang (Ying-K'ou), proclaiming that thousands of boats bringing down the produce stored in the depots mentioned above. . . . Some years ago it was estimated that 13,000 boats, varying in capacity from 7 1/7 to 14 2/7 tons, were engaged in this carrying trade, and that each boat made eight trips on an average during the season, bringing down export beans, grain, tobacco, hemp and other produce, and taking back salt, old iron and general cargo. . . . Today, owing to the enormous development of trade in Manchuria during the last few years, it may be stated with perfect safety that they number not less than 20,000 and every year even the most unobservant eye cannot fail to detect the large admixture of new craft.

According to his investigation, export trade in 1899

through Newchang (a port in South Manchuria) amounted to £3,783,915 (about $18,500,000), a tremendous figure for an allegedly "uninhabited and undeveloped" country over thirty years ago!

The Chinese *Imperial Maritime Customs Decennial Reports for 1882–1891 and 1892–1901,* commented on conditions in Manchuria for the year 1881—twenty-four years before Japan entered Manchuria:

> Anyone who could have visited Newchang during the last two months of the open season, that is, in October and November, would have been struck by the enormous quantity of shipping in the harbor, and would have argued therefrom that trade was in a flourishing condition, and that the place itself was in a most prosperous state. Arrivals occurred day after day in uninterrupted succession, until the harbour presented to the eye a perfect forest of masts.

According to those reports, the total trade for 1899 through Newchang amounted to Haikuan Tael 48,258,660 (about $39,000,000). For the same year, the population estimate was from 15,000,000 to 25,000,000 people, about 90% of which were Chinese (the number of Japanese residents was 72).

Therefore the official Chinese documents and the investigations of Sir Alexander Hosie correspond on two main points: (1) that South Manchuria had already become as early as 1882 an important trade center and a most prosperous section of China; and (2) that over thirty years ago there was already a fairly large population in Manchuria.

CHAPTER II

ENTER JAPAN AND RUSSIA

About forty years ago Japan and Russia each decided that Manchuria would be desirable for its scheme of expansion. Since then there has been no peace. Manchuria has become the cockpit but the cocks were uninvited. "The cradle of conflict" now holds the offspring of foreign parentage, because the imperialistic schemes that gave birth to the conflict were made in Tokyo and St. Petersburg.

From the Opium War in 1838 to the end of the last century, the great powers of Europe were scrambling for concessions and special privileges in China. Theretofore, Japan had been a disciple of China in her civilization. She soon became, however, an able follower of the political ideas and methods of nineteenth-century Europe. Colonial empires were the highest political aspirations and conquest was the glory of nations. From the time of the Meiji Reform, Japan, once a self-contained oriental nation, began to see new visions and dream new dreams. She entered the game of imperialism with the energy and enthusiasm of a novice, and her marked-out prey became Manchuria.

Japanese Aggressions Began in 1894

A large part of Korea's misfortunes have been due to its location; it lies between Japan and Manchuria. In ancient times the northern part of Korea was part of the Chinese Empire. In the Chou dynasty (1122-250 B.C.) it was named Chaohsien, or Chosen. It is recorded in Chinese history that Chi-Tze migrated with a group of Chinese people to that province. This gave rise to the tradition that Chi-Tze founded the Hermit Kingdom. It is certain that toward the end of the Chou dynasty there existed a large Chinese colony in northern Korea. The Korean family names, and the fact that Taoism has been the national religion of Korea, bear witness to the strong traditional ties between the two nations.

Prior to 1895, Korea had been under the suzerainty of China. The relations between the two countries had become especially cordial since the Ming dynasty. Each had come to the other's assistance in times of distress. When China was greatly weakened by her defeat in the Opium War and by the Taiping Rebellion, Japan began to interfere with Korea's internal affairs. In 1894 a rebellion broke out in Korea. The Korean Emperor requested assistance from China for its suppression. Japan claimed that she had equal right to send her forces to Korea and refused to recognize China's suzerainty. China and Japan went to war and China was defeated. The Treaty of Shimonoseki was concluded. It contains the following conditions: (1) recognition by China of the independence of Korea; (2) China's cession of southeastern Manchuria including the Liaotung Peninsula and Formosa and the Pescadores Islands; (3) China to pay to Japan an indemnity of Taels 200,000,000; (4) conclusion of a new treaty of commerce and the opening to commerce of seven cities and the right of inland navigation by Japan;

(5) temporary occupation by Japan of Mukden and Wei-heiwei.

The cession of Liaotung Peninsula would have given Japan the dominating position in North China. The balance of power in the Far East would have been disturbed. Russia intervened with the support of France and Germany. Japan was persuaded to return Liaotung Peninsula for the price of Taels 30,000,000 to be paid by China.

H. G. Moulton, President of the Brookings Institute, in his book "Japan" gives the official statistics of the Japanese Government on the cost and profit of the Sino-Japanese War,

	Yen
Net profit	200,476,000
War indemnity received	159,524,000
Expenditures	360,000,000

In addition to the net profit in cash, Japan secured the islands of Formosa and the Pescadores. The former is especially rich in natural resources.

The Sino-Japanese War revealed Japan's intentions in no uncertain terms. Russia, taking advantage of China's fear of another attempt by Japan to take South Manchuria, pretended to be friendly and offered to assist in defending China in case of another Japanese attack. The Li-Lobanov defensive alliance was concluded in 1896 immediately after China's defeat. The Chinese Eastern Railway was built under the joint control of the two countries in 1896 and the Liaotung Peninsula was leased to Russia in 1898.

Soon Russia proved to be a second Japan. She not only broke the agreement one year after it was made, but also took advantage of China's internal conditions illegally and forcibly to extend her control in Manchuria.

Meantime, Japan was preparing for a second attempt to seize "the land of promise." In 1904 she challeged the position of Russia in Manchuria by declaring war on Russia.

Throughout the Russo-Japanese War, China maintained strict neutrality. The war, which lasted for about a year, was fought on Chinese territory and resulted in heavy losses in Chinese lives and property. Japan did not score a decisive victory. According to Felix Morley, "Contrary to popular impression, this war was by no means the sweeping victory for Japan that has been pictured. The Japanese delegates to the Portsmouth Peace Conference faced the Russians not as dictators, but as negotiators fully conscious that continuation of hostilities might see the tide of battle turn against them."

Under the Treaty of Portsmouth of 1905, Japan finally gained a foothold in South Manchuria. She secured the transfer of the rights of Russia in the Liaotung Peninsula, including the two important harbors, Dairen and Port Arthur, and the control of the southern section of the Chinese Eastern Railway, which ran through the richest section of Manchuria.

Without a decisive victory, Japan had reached the objective of the previous war with China. Moreover, Japan secured recognition from Russia and China of her special political and military position in Korea. Thus she prepared the way to seize that country five years later.

Origin of Japanese Rationalizations

It is interesting to compare here history and later Japanese rationalizations of history. One of them is that Japan fought Russia to preserve the integrity of China. She apparently had not thought of the integrity of China in the Sino-Japanese War. When Japan declared war on Russia in 1904, she solemnly announced that "the integrity and independence of Korea is a matter of deep concern to this Empire." Hardly one year before the annexation, Prince Ito declared in behalf of the Japanese Emperor that, "The annexation of Korea has no part in the purpose of the Japanese Government." Japan annexed Korea in 1910, and, since then, has held the Korean people in subjugation under her iron heel. These facts do not seem to bear out her declarations of "self-denial" and "sacrificial" motives. The war did cost Japan many *yen* and many lives, but such is the price of imperialistic glory!

CHAPTER III

JAPAN CLOSES THE OPEN DOOR

AFTER Japan entered South Manchuria she largely closed the door to other nations.

She did this contrary to the principles of the Open Door which Japan repeatedly professed, and her pledge in the Treaty of Portsmouth—

Article IV—Japan and Russia reciprocally engage not to obstruct any general measures, common to all countries, which China may take for the development of the commerce and industry of Manchuria.

In an article entitled "Economic Effect of the Extension of Japan's Spheres of Influence in China," published May 1915, George Bronson Rea, editor of the *Far Eastern Review* wrote:

Experience has shown that any regions in China in which political control is exercised by the Japanese, the tendency is for foreign trade other than Japanese to diminish. . . . It can be seen from the figures . . . that Japanese goods even when there was some limitation to the control exercised by Japan over South Manchuria, succeeded in displacing those from other countries. When we turn to Korea . . . it is found that the trade of other countries, other than Japan is steadily diminishing. . . . When it is found that in one region in China in which the Japanese exercise political control and influence the trade of European and American nations succumbs to Japanese state-aided attacks, it is fair to assume that similar results

13

will follow the acquisition of special interests of Japan in other localities. Japan desires to extend her political influence over Eastern Inner Mongolia, Shangtung, Fukien. . . . Some Japanese publicists are quite candid in regard to Japan's ambitions. They state that Japan is sufficiently powerful to compel the European and American merchants to surrender the China market to exclusive Japanese exploitation. Japan professes belief in the Open Door policy as long as she thinks it advantageous for her to do so, but the time, they declare, has come when Japan can disclose her real policy, that of exclusion. . . .

Stanley K. Hornbeck now of the State Department of the United States, wrote in "Contemporary Politics in the Far East," published in 1916:

That the tariff of the South Manchuria Railway did and does discriminate against the port of Newchang in favor of Dairen no one denies. That there was inaugurated a system of rebates of which, in the nature of things, only Japanese could take advantage, and that, in view of the volume of complaint against it, the Japanese government abolished this system in September 1909, is a matter of common knowledge. That the Railway and the Yokohama Specie Bank have devised a system of handling the produce of the country which brings practically all of the bean business into their hands—a system which is to their credit and to the advantage of the Manchurian farmers—has been pointed to as another instance of the governmental participation in a field of activity which is usually left to private enterprise. That the Japanese banks advance money at unusually low rates of interest has occasioned adverse comment—a criticism which would not be warranted but for the facts that a distinction is made in favor of Japanese borrowers and that the Japanese government gives the banks special assistance which makes it possible for them to carry on business in this way. . . .

Now to turn to an instance or two of practices whose effect is more direct: Before the war the tobacco trade in Manchuria was largely in the hands of the British-American Tobacco Company. When the Japanese government compelled the company to sell to it its factories in Japan, the company began the erection of factories in China. The Japanese Government Tobacco Monopoly soon became a serious competitor of the British-American Company, particularly in Manchuria. After the war, artificial obstacles were placed in the way of the business of the latter. For instance, the return of its agents was delayed; the hawkers of its products were interfered with in the railway zone; and the trade-marks of the company were imitated.

International Development of Railways Blocked by Japan

In 1907 the Chinese Government contracted with a British firm, Pauling and Company, to build a short line of about 50 miles from Hsinmintun to Fakumen for the development of Western Manchuria, financed by a loan to the Chinese government from a joint Chinese and British Corporation. This firm had the original contract, signed in 1898, to build railways in that section. Japan brought pressure upon the Chinese and British governments and successfully blocked the carrying out of this project, and contended that, if the line should be built, it must be a feeder of the Japanese system.

The so-called "Knox Plan" was formulated upon a preliminary agreement between the Chinese government, the British contractors, and an American banking group, for the construction of a line to connect the Peiping-Mukden Railway at Chinchow with Aigun, a Chinese city of the Amur River in the northern part of Manchuria. Mr. Willard Straight represented the American group of bankers which included J. P. Morgan & Company, Kuhn, Loeb & Company, the First National Bank, and the National City Bank of New York. This plan became known as the "Knox Plan" because the Secretary of State of the American government, Mr. Knox, proposed, in support of this project, the neutralization of the Manchurian railways so that other countries, including the United States, might have an equal opportunity to develop the railways in Manchuria under a unified and scientific management. Secretary Knox apparently presumed that both Russia and Japan professed the Open Door principle in good faith and did not take the trouble of sounding out in advance the attitude of those two powers towards this project. When the proposal was made known in November, 1909, Russia, in constant touch with the Japanese government, took the leadership in rejecting the proposal. The "Knox Plan" failed.

It is significant that, in objecting to the proposal, Japan did not even mention any special reason, not even her pretext of contending that the projected line was "parallel" or competitive to her system. The Japanese minister bluntly warned the Chinese government that if China did not heed the combined warning of Japan and Russia, "serious trouble" might follow.

Soon after the establishment of the Chinese Republic, the Chinese government planned the economic development of Manchuria. The great powers were sympathetic and organized the Four-Power Consortium. The Chinese government intended to secure loans from this Consortium in order to develop the railways and resources in Manchuria and also to prepare herself to redeem the Russian and Japanese railway leases when they should mature. In 1911 Japan made the following declaration:

Japan possesses in the region of Southern Manchuria special rights and interests and while she is fully prepared in the future, as in the past, to respect the rights of others, she is unable to view with indifference measures which tend not only to menace those special rights and interests, but to place her subjects and institutions at a disadvantage as compared with the subjects and institutions of any other country.

The next year Russia made a similar declaration, asserting that she had special rights and interests in the regions of Northern Manchuria, Mongolia, and Western Manchuria. Both Japan and Russia managed to join the Consortium, with reservations of their special rights and also attaching political significance to the terms under which the Consortium was to function. This compelled the United States to withdraw from the Consortium in 1913, declaring "Our interests are those of the Open Door—a door of friendship and mutual advantage. This is the only door we care to enter."

Attempt to Commit the United States

The presentation of the Twenty-One Demands by Japan in 1915 aroused nation-wide reaction in the United States. Therefore, Japan decided to send a special mission to win back American confidence and to secure America's recognition of her special rights and position in Manchuria. In 1917 the Japanese government sent Count Ishii as Envoy Extraordinary and Minister Plenipotentiary to the United States and concluded an understanding that same year with Secretary of State Lansing. It is difficult to ascertain the real meaning and motive of Japan in obtaining this understanding. The Japanese sought to claim that the United States in the agreement recognized Japan's special interest and position in Manchuria, which superseded the Open

Door principle. The American interpretation has been different. The agreement caused so much misunderstanding that it was terminated in 1923. Since then Japan has persisted in attempting to have the United States government recognize her special position in Manchuria.

Japan's intentions were disclosed at a hearing before the United States Senate Committee on Foreign Relations in 1917:

SENATOR BORAH: He (Ishii) said that his idea was that Japan had special interests in China which right was to be recognized, and by those interests he meant paramount control?

SECRETARY LANSING: Yes; and I told him I could not consider it.

. . . . .

SENATOR BRANDAGEE: Did he at any time intimate that it meant paramountcy or interest different from that of any other nation, other than from Japan's propinquity to China?

SECRETARY LANSING: My only recollection as to that is that he wishes to have inserted the words "special interests and influence" and I objected seriously to the insertion of the words "and influence" and they were stricken out.

SENATOR BORAH: In view of the Twenty-One Demands, what construction did you place upon the question of Japan's special interest in China?

SECRETARY LANSING: Only the special interest that comes from being contiguous to another country whose peace and prosperity were involved.

SENATOR BORAH: No different special interest from that which we have in Canada?

SECRETARY LANSING: No.

CHAPTER IV

JAPAN ESTABLISHES ECONOMIC AND POLITICAL DOMINATION

FROM the very beginning, Japan was determined to establish her dominant economic and political position in South Manchuria. She accomplished her purposes by (1) developing her railway system for political and strategic purposes, and (2) by establishing railway monopoly and preventing China from developing a railway system of her own.

Three agencies were set up by the Japanese Government for economic and political control.

1. The South Railway Company for economic and financial control.
2. The Government of the Kwantung Leased Territory for political control.
3. The Kwantung Garrison for military control.

All three agencies are mutually independent. The Governor General of Kwantung Leased Territory is appointed by the Japanese Emperor. Japanese consular officials who perform political and jurisdictional powers in Manchuria are under the Government of the Kwantung Leased Territory and not the Foreign Office. The Commander of the Japanese Garrison in Manchuria is under the War Department. All three agencies are directly responsible to the Japanese Emperor.

The South Manchuria Railway Company

No more incorrect conception can be made of the Manchurian situation than to think that the South Manchuria Railway Company is purely a commercial concern. It is no more a commercial concern than was the famous British East India Company which made India a colony of England. That the Company is practically a Japanese government bureau is proved by the different Imperial Ordinances that created the Company:

The President and Vice President shall be appointed by the Japanese Government.

The Japanese Government shall appoint directors from among the shareholders.

The Japanese Government shall have the power to supervise the business of the company and to dismiss the officers.

The Governor-General of Kwantung (a Japanese government official) shall have charge of the operation and protection (by military force if necessary) of the railways of the company.

The Company not only operates directly and indirectly iron and coal mines, an oil shale and utilization plant, a harbor, and a steamship line, but also controls public service in a wide area. It has electric power stations in more than four cities, tramways in two, gas plants in six, and waterworks in seventeen cities.

The political and military administrations of the Japanese Government in Manchuria usurp the functions of the Chinese Government in performing the function of taxation and in stationing one division and sixteen battalions of troops along the railway. They have acquired for themselves an *imperium in imperio*.

The extension of their authority and jurisdiction is, in itself, a direct violation of the Treaty of Portsmouth which contains the following provisions:

> Article III—Japan and Russia mutually engage:
> 1. To evacuate completely and simultaneously Manchuria except the territory affected by the lease of the Liaotung Peninsula, in conformity with the provisions of additional Article I annexed to Treaty.
> 2. To restore entirely and completely to the exclusive administration of China all portions of Manchuria now in the occupation or under the control of the Japanese or Russian troops, with the exception of the territory above mentioned.
>
> Article VII—Japan and Russia engage to exploit their respective railways in Manchuria exclusively for commercial and industrial purposes and in no wise for strategic purposes.

The additional agreements to the Sino-Japanese Treaty of December 22, 1905, contain the following:

> Article II—In view of the earnest desire expressed by the Imperial Chinese Government to have the Japanese and Russian troops and railway guards in Manchuria withdrawn as soon as possible, and in order to meet this desire, the Imperial Japanese Government, in the event of Russia agreeing to the withdrawal of her railway guards, or in case other proper measures are agreed to between China and Russia, consent to take similar steps accordingly, . . .

Russian troops have been withdrawn long since. Japanese troops have remained.

Japan intended to make, and, to a large extent, has succeeded in making, her railway system the main artery of land transportation that connects with her port of Dairen. She also plans to link her railways in Korea to North Manchuria and West Manchuria so that in case of war she can strike speedily and effectively at Peiping and Tientsin and strategic points in Siberia.

Conspiracy With Russia

In order to prevent China from developing a railway system of her own, Japan concluded a secret agreement with Russia in 1907 in which Russia recognized her spheres of influence in Inner Mongolia, South Manchuria, and Korea, while Japan, on her part, recognized Russia's special interest in Outer Mongolia and Northern Manchuria. Japan and Russia confirmed this demarkation in July 1910 and further pledged cooperation between their railway systems in Manchuria and the maintenance of the status quo. The real significance of these two agreements is that the two powers agreed to prevent the development of railways by China and other powers.

Commenting on this conspiracy between Russia and Japan, Stanley K. Hornbeck wrote in "Contemporary Politics in the Far East"—

To disinterested observers who have followed the course of events in Manchuria, with Russia in the north and Japan in the south, the two working now separately, now together, the evidences lead to but one conclusion: that these two countries are bent upon the absorption of that region. Whether it is to be divided between them or all to be taken by one of them, or whether China will be able to retain a part, remains for time to tell. The Russian and the Japanese governments, though pledged to both, approve of neither of the two fundamental principles of American policy in the Far East—the Open Door and the integrity of China.

Secretary of State Knox of the United States proposed, on November 6, 1909, that "to preserve the undisturbed enjoyment of China of all political rights in Manchuria and to promote development of those provinces under a practical application of the Open Door and equal commercial opportunity—

(1), The most effective way . . . would be to bring the Manchurian highways, the railroads, under an economic, scientific, and impartial administration by some plan vesting in China the ownership of the railroads through funds furnished for that purpose by the interested powers willing to participate.

(2), Should this suggestion not be found feasible in its entirety, then the desired end would be approximated, if not attained, by Great Britain and the United States diplomatically supporting the Chinchou-Aigun arrangement and inviting the interested friendly powers to complete commercial neutralization of Manchuria, to participate in the financing and construction of that line and of such additional lines as future commercial development may demand and at the same time to supply funds for the purchase by China of such of the existing lines as might be offered for inclusion in this system.

Japan and Russia promptly rejected the proposal. The following warning was sent by the Japanese Foreign Minister to the Chinese Government on January 31, 1910:

Before the Chinese Government determines anything, the consent of my Government must first be obtained. If the position of my Government is ignored, it will be hard to estimate the seriousness of the trouble that may be caused in the relations of the two countries.

The Alleged Secret Protocol

Thus, Japan made herself the dictator of railway building in Manchuria. In order to give some legal semblance to her dictatorship she alleges that there exists some such treaty-agreement as follows:

The Chinese Government engage, for the purpose of protecting the interest of the South Manchurian Railway, not to construct, prior to the recovery by them of the said railway, any main line in the neighborhood of and parallel to that railway, or any branch line which might be prejudicial to the interest of the above-mentioned railway.

W. W. Rockhill, Special Commissioner of the United States to China at the time, wrote about the Protocol in "Treaties and Conventions With or Concerning China and Korea"—

Tang Shao-yi, Governor of Fengtien, who signed the Peking Agreement, categorically denied the existence of the clause debarring China from paralleling the South Manchurian Railway. Tang Shao-yi further gave distinct assurance that there was no secret agreement between Japan and China and that all the Legations had been apprized of this fact upon the conclusion of the Komura negotiations. Tang Shao-yi intimated that an agreement that China should not parallel the Japanese railroad had been sought and discussed, but not made, and implied that such discussion appeared in the signed minutes of the conference, the inference being that there was absolutely no agreement, but simply an evidence of discussion on this subject.

Since that time the authenticity of the Protocol has never been ascertained. In his authoritative work—"Japan's Special Position in Manchuria," published in November 1931, C. Walter Young writes:

At the outset, it is evident that when the ratifications of the Sino-Japanese treaty and additional agreement of December 22, 1905, were exchanged (January 23, 1906), no additional "Protocols" or other commitments were at the same time included in the instrument of ratification. Nor is there evidence of subsequent formal ratification of such "Protocols." It is conspicuous that where the treaty and additional agreement of 1905 appear in the official Japanese Foreign Treaty collection, there is no version, either in French, Japanese or Chinese, or any other language, of such "Protocols."

Even if such a protocol existed, great injustices have been done to China because Japan has insisted that she alone has the right to define what is meant by "neighborhood" and "parallel."

Extension of the Railway "Zone"

The Japanese Government has employed force and other illegal methods to acquire mines and lands along her railways over which she has extended jurisdiction. The way the Japanese have acquired lands after the Russo-Japanese War left a deep impression upon the minds of the Chinese people.

In 1902, two Chinese merchants each secured a concession from the Government to work the coal deposits of Fushun. Later one of them, Mr. Wang, admitted $60,000 Mexican from the Russo-Chinese Bank as shares in his enterprise. Still later, he bought out the right of the other Chinese and applied to the central Government through the Military Governor of Fengtien for incorporation. The Board of Foreign Affairs, in view of the foreign interests involved, advised the Military Governor to apply for special permission from the throne. The matter was not settled when the Russo-Japanese War broke out. The mines were first occupied by the Russians and then by the Japanese. After the War, on the petition of the concessionaire, Mr. Wang, the Board of Foreign Affairs communicated with the Japanese Minister, requesting their restoration. The Japanese Government held that the property in question was Russian and hence should pass over to Japan by virtue of Article VI of the Portsmouth Treaty. At the same time, Japan proceeded to occupy three more coal mines 10 *li* from Fushun worked by other Chinese, who had nothing to do with the Chinese Eastern Railway.

A similar case happened at Yentai. There were four coal beds worked by some private Russian merchants and three by Chinese, when the Japanese troops reached the Yentai district. The Russian beds were closed down, but the Chinese were left in operation after some examination by the Japanese commander. In July, 1906, after the organization of the South Manchurian Railway Company was ordained, the Japanese suddenly took possession of two of the Chinese beds. The Military Governor took up the case with the Japanese Consul-General at Mukden. As the Chinese Eastern Railway was not involved in this case, the Japanese justified their action by Article VI of the agreement relating to the South Manchurian branch, in which China granted the Company the right to mine such coal as might be needed for the construction and operation of the railway. Regardless of the Chinese contention that the article cited did not give Japan the exclusive right, but definitely contemplated "other parties" as well, Japan determined unilaterally to make the Yentai and the Fushun mines the exclusive properties of the South Manchurian Railway, whereupon the Government order of August, 1906, assigned them to the Company. (Lin Tung-chi in "Political Aspects of the Japanese Railway Enterprise in Manchuria"—*The Chinese Social and Political Science Review*, April, 1930.)

APPENDIX TO CHAPTER IV

How Japan Established Exclusive Economic Control in Manchuria

(A Chronological Summary)

I. Exclusive Right of Investment

1907–1910—Japan prevented the United States and Great Britain from making a loan to China for railway construction.

    1. The Hsimintun-Fakumen Railway project.

    2. The Knox Plan.

    3. The Chinchow-Aigun Railway project.

1911   —Japan and Russia versus the United States, Germany, France, Great Britain, and China.

    1. The Consortium: Japan and Russia claimed special interests in Mongolia and Manchuria in priority of investment and imposed political conditions on loans to be made by the Consortium.

    2. Currency reform and Manchurian industrial development loan blocked by Russia and Japan.

1915   —Japan versus China and the United States.

        1. Japan claims priority of investment in Inner Mongolia and Manchuria under the Twenty-One Demands. The United States refused to recognize any treaty that contravened the Open Door.

        2. Illegal political loans by Japan.

1918–1920—Japan versus the United States, France, Great Britain, and China.

        1. Formation of a new Consortium and pooling of all rights and options.

        2. The new Consortium has not been able to function due to Japanese obstruction.

II. Establishment of Railway Monopoly

1905   —Claim of the "secret protocol."

1907   —Japan blocked the Pauling and Company (a British firm) railway project. Japan bound China to apply to Japan if foreign loans were needed to construct the Changchun-Kirin Railway.

1909   —Japan claimed the right to finance the construction of railway line to Huening.

1909–1910—Japan blocks the Chinchow-Aigun railway project of the United States and Great Britain.

1913   —Japan obtains a provisional agreement to finance the construction of the following railways:

        Ssupingkai-Taonan

        Kaiyan-Hailungcheng

        Changchun-Taonan

        Taonan-Jehol

        Kirin-Hailungcheng

        Connecting line between Taonan-Jehol Railway and a seaport (Hulutao).

1915   —Japan claimed priority to finance the construction of all railways in South Manchuria and Inner Mongolia (part of the Twenty-One Demands).

1920   —Japan's reservation of the right to finance the construction of seven proposed lines in the new Consortium agreement.

1921–22—Japan made reservations about Manchuria at the Washington Conference.

1927–1928—Japan opposed the construction of the Tahushan-Paiyantalai Railway and the development of Hulutao harbor.

CHAPTER V

THE TWENTY-ONE DEMANDS

So far we have seen how Japan entered South Manchuria, how she closed the Open Door, and how she built up her dominant political and economic position by preventing China and other powers from developing Manchuria, especially by railways. During 1905 to 1915 she had made herself master. The so-called railway "zone," originally a right-of-way of from 50 to 300 feet on either side of the tracks, had been extended to include mines, forests and several municipalities with Japanese schools and police and administered by Japanese officials. In other words, the "zone" had become a part of the Japanese Empire in practically everything but name. It was for the purpose of "rubber-stamping" what she had illegally acquired and to obtain a "treaty-basis" for what she intended to acquire that the Twenty-One Demands were presented in 1915.

The Treaty of Portsmouth of 1905 transferred to Japan the control of the southern part of the Chinese Eastern Railway and the lease of the Liaotung Peninsula including Port Arthur and Dairen. Her rights in South Manchuria rest on the original Russian lease, which would have expired in 1923. The Sino-Japanese Agreement of December 22, 1905, under which the Mukden-Antung Railway was built specifically states:

The term of the concession above mentioned is therefore to expire in the 49th year of Kuang-Hsu (i.e. in 1923).

Since 1923 Japan has rested her claim to retain the control of the railway and the leased territory on the validity of the "1915 Treaties" which resulted from the Twenty-One Demands.

In 1915 the rest of the world was preoccupied with the European War. China had become a republic only four years before. It was an opportune time for Japan to strike. Paul S. Reinsch, then American Minister in Peking in his book "An American Diplomat in China" quoted the Japanese Minister to China, Hioki, who said in 1015:

> The present crisis throughout the world virtually forces my Government to take far-reaching action. . . . When there is fire in a jewelry shop the neighbors cannot be expected to refrain from helping themselves.

The Extraordinary Circumstances

Stanley K. Hornbeck comments in his book, "Contemporary Politics in the Far East":

> Japan's methods in connection with the presentation of the Demands, and the manner in which she prosecuted the negotiations which ensued, antagonized the Chinese and provoked criticism from every quarter—including even a significantly critical opposition in Japan. To begin with, there was no particular justification for the making of the Demands. China had done nothing against Japan; there had been no war and there was no particular contention between the two countries. In presenting the Demands, the Japanese Minister went directly to the President of China, which is contrary to diplomatic usage. Then, the Japanese demanded of China secrecy and did their utmost to keep the world uninformed as to the content and character of the Demands. When finally the news leaked out,

information came from China to the effect that twenty-one demands had been made, and a precis of the content of the demands was made available. The Japanese declared to the world that only eleven demands had been made. Japanese publicists and Japanese apologists all over the world asserted that China was misrepresenting the substance of the demands. The public was instructed to believe no reports except those which emanated from Tokyo; above all, to pay no attention to news from Peking; it was impossible that Japan could think of taking advantage of China or of doing anything other than scrupulously observing her treaty pledges. Ultimately, the documentary evidence showed that the Peking account of the demands was the true version.

Briefly described, the Twenty-One Demands were as follows:

Group I—Demands of railway, mining and concession rights in Shantung.

Group II—Extension to 99 years of leases of Port Arthur, Dairen, the South Manchurian Railway, and the Antung-Mukden Railway, the management and control of the Kirin-Changchun Railway for 99 years; and other exclusive railway and mining rights, and priority in investments.

Group III—The control of China's main source of iron and coal supply in Central China.

Group IV—Dealt with the entire coast of China.

Group V—Demands that China should have Japanese police and that China should employ Japanese advisers in financial, political, and military affairs.

Five months before, the Premier of Japan had made the declaration that "Japan has no ulterior motive, no desire to secure more territory, no thought of depriving China or other people of anything which they now possess"!

Under Group II Japan demanded an extension of all her leases and rights in South Manchuria to ninety-nine years as shown by the following table:

	Original Expiration in	Extension demanded 99 years from	to Year
Kwantung leased territory	1923	1898	1997
Antung-Mukden Railway	1923	1908	2007
South Manchurian Railway main line redeemable in	1939	1903	2002

Group V again proves beyond doubt Japan's real intentions. Hornbeck comments further—

The most astonishing of the demands of this group were those regarding police and the purchase or manufacture of arms. The granting of the first of these would connote an extensive abrogation of sovereign rights, would imply a consciousness on China's part of inability to administer her own affairs, and would inevitably lead to acute and intolerable friction. The granting of the second would involve a more conspicuous disregard of the principles of equal opportunity in China's markets than has ever in a single instance been shown. It would necessitate China's making familiar to Japan every detail of her military preparations and equipment, thus substantially subordinating herself in these vitally important matters to the will and convenience of Japan. The two together would, in the course of a few years, not only put China absolutely at the mercy of Japan but would produce conditions to which Japan could point as ample justification for such measures as she might choose to take for the ostensible purpose of removing those conditions. If China assented to these, along with the other demands, she would be assigning herself as a protectorate, immediately to Japan.

Contrary to popular impression, the "1915 Agreements" resulting from the Twenty-One Demands have never been cancelled. Japan has consistently refused to discuss the question at any international conference. The Japanese government has even since maintained the position that these agreements constitute valid treaties under which she has retained the control of the leased territory and the railways. When the Japanese government speaks of the sanctity of treaties and of China's violation of her treaty rights, it has particularly in mind the so-called "1915 Agreements."

The Validity of the "1915 Agreements"

Whether the "1915 Agreements" resulted from the Twenty-One Demands are valid is open to question. Those who think in the affirmative have to rely entirely on technicality. Even so, the manner and circumstances in which they were presented are without parallel in the history of international relations. The Chinese signature to the document was secured by an ultimatum backed by force. The so-called treaties were never ratified by any Chinese legislative body. On the contrary, on many occasions successive Chinese governments have declared them to be fundamentally null and void. Above all, the agreements resulting from the Twenty-One Demands contravene all principles of international justice and, especially, the principles of the Open Door and the Nine Power Treaty, in that they provide for exclusive rights and political domination for Japan and that they jeopardize the territorial integrity and administrative independence of China.

They were not made at the conclusion of a war as the price of victory. Though concluded in time of complete peace, Japan neither paid nor offered to pay a quid pro quo of any character.

Many authorities believe that the "1915 Agreements" are invalid because they are unjust and constitute a direct violation of the inherent rights of the Chinese people. W. E. Hall in "A Treatise on International Law" writes, "Therefore, a treaty becomes voidable as soon as it is dangerous to the life of or incompatible with the independence of the state." It is impossible for China to recognize the fundamental validity of the "1915 Agreements" without endangering her status as an independent nation. On account of the extremely unethical and inequitable character of the 1915 dictated "Agreements" the Chinese government has repeatedly sought for an equitable solution of the situation they have created.

Technically, international law does not always invalidate a treaty signed under duress. But unjust treaties are like unjust laws. They invariably lead to strife and war.

APPENDIX TO CHAPTER V

Chinese Statement at the Washington Conference

February 3, 1922

The Chinese delegation has taken note of the statement of Baron Shidehara made at yesterday's session of the Committee with reference to the Sino-Japanese Treaties and Notes of May 25, 1915.

The Chinese delegation learns with satisfaction that Japan is now ready to throw open to the joint activity of the banking interests of other Powers the right of option granted exclusively in favour of Japanese capital with regard, first, to loans for the construction of railways in South Manchuria and Eastern Inner Mongolia and, second, to loans secured on taxes in that region; and that Japan has no intention of insisting upon a preferential right concerning the engagement by China of Japanese advisers or instructors in political, financial, military or police matters in South Manchuria; also that Japan now withdraws the reservation which she made to the effect that group 5 of her original demands upon China should be postponed for future negotiations.

The Chinese delegation greatly regrets that the Government of Japan should not have been led to renounce the other claims predicated upon the Treaties and Notes of 1915.

The Japanese delegation expressed the opinion that abrogation of these arguments would constitute "an exceedingly dangerous precedent," "with far-reaching consequences upon the stability of the existing international relations in Asia, in Europe, and everywhere."

The Chinese delegation has the honour to say that a still more dangerous precedent will be established, with consequences upon the stability of international relations which cannot be estimated if, without rebuke or protest from other Powers, one nation can obtain from a friendly but, in a military sense, weaker neighbour, and under circumstances such as attended the negotiation and signing of the Treaties of 1915, valuable concessions which were not in satisfaction of pending controversies and for which no quid pro quo was offered. These treaties and notes stand out, indeed, unique in the annals of international relations. History records scarcely another instance in which demands of such a serious character as those which Japan presented to China in 1915 have, without even pretence of provocation, been suddenly presented by one nation to another nation with which it was at the time in friendly relations.

No apprehension need be entertained that the abrogation of the agreements of 1915 will serve as a precedent for the annulment of other agreements, since it is confidently hoped that the future will furnish no such similar occurrences.

So exceptional were the conditions under which the agreements of 1915 were negotiated that the Government of the United States of America felt justified in referring to them in the identic note of May 13th, 1915, which it sent to the Chinese and Japanese Governments. That note began with the statement that, "in view of the circumstances of the negotiations which have taken place and which are now pending between the Government of China and the Government of Japan and of the agreements which have been reached as the result thereof, the Government of the United States has the honour to notify the Government of the Chinese Republic (Japan) that it cannot recognize any agreement or undertaking which has been entered into between the Governments of China and Japan impairing the treaty rights of the United States and its citizens in

China, the political or territorial integrity of the Republic of China, or the international policy relative to China commonly known as the 'Open-Door Policy.' "

Conscious of her obligations to the other Powers, the Chinese Government, immediately after signing the agreements, published a formal statement protesting against the agreements which she had been compelled to sign, and disclaiming responsibility for consequent violations of treaty rights of the other Powers. In the statement thus issued, the Chinese Government declared that, although it was "constrained to comply in full with the terms of the (Japanese) ultimatum" it nevertheless "disclaims any desire to associate itself with any revision, which may be thus effected, of the various conventions and agreements concluded between the other Powers in respect of the maintenance of China's territorial independence and integrity, the preservation of the status quo and the principle of equal opportunity for the commerce and industry of all nations in China."

Because of the essential injustice of these provisions, the Chinese delegation, acting on behalf of the Chinese Government and of the Chinese people, has felt itself in duty bound to present to this Conference, representing the Powers with substantial interests in the Far East, the question as to the equity and justice of these agreements and therefore as to their fundamental validity.

If Japan is disposed to rely solely upon a claim as to the technical or juristic validity of the agreements of 1915, as having been actually signed in due form by the two Governments, it may be said that, so far as this Conference is concerned, the contention is largely irrelevant, for this gathering of the representatives of the nine Powers has not had for its purpose the maintenance of the legal status quo. Upon the contrary, the purpose has been, if possible, to bring about such changes in existing conditions upon the Pacific and in the Far East as might be expected to promote that enduring friendship among the nations which the President of the United States spoke of in his letter of invitation to the Powers to participate in this Conference.

For the following reasons, therefore, the Chinese delegation is of the opinion that the Sino-Japanese Treaties and Exchange of Notes of May 25th, 1915, should form the subject of impartial examination with a view to their abrogation:

1. In exchange for the concessions demanded of China, Japan offered no quid pro quo. The benefits derived from the agreements were wholly unilateral.

2. The agreements, in important respects, are in violation of treaties between China and the other Powers.

3. The agreements are inconsistent with the principles relating to China which have been adopted by the Conference.

4. The agreements have engendered constant misunderstanding between China and Japan, and, if not abrogated, will necessarily tend, in the future, to disturb friendly relations between the two countries, and will thus constitute an obstacle in the way of realizing the purpose for the attainment of which this Conference was convened. As to this, the Chinese delegation, by way of conclusion, can perhaps do no better than quote from a resolution introduced in the Japanese Parliament, in June 1915, by Mr. Hara, later Premier of Japan, a resolution which received the support of some one hundred and thirty of the members of the parliament.

The resolution reads:

> *Resolved,* that the negotiations carried on with China by the present Government have been inappropriate in every respect; that they are detrimental to the amicable relationship between the two countries, and provocative of suspicions on the part of the Powers; that they have the effect of lowering the prestige of the Japanese Empire; and that, while far from capable of establishing the foundation of peace in the Far East, they will form the source of future trouble.

The foregoing declaration has been made in order that the Chinese Government may have upon record the view which it takes, and will continue to take, regarding the Sino-Japanese Treaties and Exchange Notes of May 25, 1915.

CHAPTER VI

PROBLEM OF POPULATION

AFTER a quarter of a century of government-encouraged immigration, less than 220,000 Japanese were in Manchuria prior to September 1931. This number is in striking contrast to the enthusiastic prediction of Premier Komura who prophesied twenty-five years ago that in ten years Japan would move 1,000,000 colonists into Manchuria. During 1911 and 1921 the Japanese Government spent an enormous sum of money to subsidize Japanese farmers to settle in Manchuria. Under this artificial stimulus a considerable number of Japanese farmers did immigrate, but as soon as the subsidy was withdrawn practically all of them returned to Japan. Most of the Japanese leaders have admitted that her policy of colonizing Manchuria has been a failure.

The population problem in Japan is not so great as Japanese publicists would have us believe. In the first place, a highly industrialized country like Japan can support many more people per square mile than an agricultural country like China. Japan may need a population outlet in the future, but, at present, her problem of over-population is not so pressing as that of China. Stanley K. Hornbeck in his "Contemporary Politics in the Far East" writes:

> Told as we have been over and over, that Japan must have an outlet for her excess population and that Manchuria is the natural outlet, it is well to bear in mind that *China also has a crowded population*. Manchuria is a natural outlet for the excess of China's popu-

lation more truly than for that of Japan; and, as far as *rights* to this open field are concerned, China has the better claim.

Another authority on Manchuria, C. Walter Young, writes in The Annals of the American Academy of Political and Social Science, November, 1930:

If there is a pressing population problem in Japan, Manchuria does not show it. Too much has been said of the impossibility of Japanese competition with Chinese . . . but the more fundamental factors are these: the disinclination of the Japanese to migrate unless under artificial stimulus; the doubtful existence of circumstances in Japan compelling migration; and finally the futility, granted the existence of a population problem, of attempting to solve it by emigration.

The Chinese people need Manchuria many times more urgently than do the Japanese. This fact is proven by the migration of an average of 500,000 Chinese refugees to Manchuria each year during the last six years. In addition to the number of permanent settlers over half a million Chinese each year from other parts of China depend on Manchuria for seasonal employment. The natural causes for famine in China have not yet been removed. It is a long and difficult engineering and agricultural process which involves reforestation, irrigation and flood control. For years to come China must depend on Manchuria for food and as a population outlet to solve her problem of famine and over-population. This region is no longer sparsely populated, being already twice as thickly settled as is the United States.

A New Japanese System

Since the annexation of Korea in 1910, Japan has been using that country as a stepping-stone to make further inroads into Manchuria. At first, Japan attempted to colonize Manchuria with her own people. When this proved a failure, Japan adopted a policy of pushing the Koreans into Manchuria and placing Japanese colonists in their places, especially in the warm and fertile regions of Korea. Professor Yoshimo of the Imperial University of Tokyo stated (in an article in the Tashchuo-Horon of Tokyo and translated into the English language in the *Japan Chronicle Weekly* of July 13, 1919), that the Japanese authorities "without consideration had mercilessly resorted to law for the expropriation of land, the Koreans concerned being compelled to part with their family property almost for nothing." The *New York Times* on January 29, 1919, reported that, as a result of this policy, one-fifth of the richest land in Korea was in the hands of Japanese in less than ten years.

Since 1919 this new method of solving the population problem has proved more successful. Thousands of Koreans have been driven out of Korea into Manchuria by various methods, one of which has been the ruthless persecution of those Koreans who participated in, or sympathized with, the Independence Movement of 1920. Consequently, the number of Koreans in Manchuria increased to about 600,000 in ten years. Incidentally, Japan finds this to be another way of solving her problem of food supplies. The Japanese government in Korea encourages rice cultivation and the exportation of as much rice as possible from Korea to Japan, while large quantities of millet have been imported from Manchuria to feed the Koreans.

CHAPTER VII

PROBLEM OF RAW MATERIALS

Agricultural Products

MANCHURIA is mainly agricultural. Its largest single resource is agricultural products.

Because of its fertile soil and favorable climate, Manchuria can always be depended upon not only to yield good harvests, but also for twenty per cent of its annual output as surplus for export. Of the five principal crops, soya beans, kao-liang, millet, maize, and wheat, soya beans are the most important as food and fertilizer. Manchuria yields about 60 per cent of the total world production of soya beans. With only about 60 per cent of its cultivable land under cultivation, it is already one of the most important food producing centers in the Far East.

Coal

Japan's need for the coal in Manchuria has been exaggerated. According to Foster H. Bain, who has made a study of "Ores and Industry in the Far East," the total coal reserve of Manchuria is only one-seventh that of Japan. "Contrary to a wide impression," writes C. Walter Young in the Annals of the American Academy of Political and Social Science, November, 1930, "Japan has a large annual home production [of coal], ranking among the first ten countries of the world. Japan is, in fact, an exporter, as well as an importer, of coal, the excess of imports being frequently caused by artificial factors in the coal industry and not by a dearth of the home product, or lack of reserves." In 1930 and 1931 Japanese coal imports and exports are about balance. This and the fact that Japan places a very heavy import duty on coal further indicates that Japan's need of coal from other countries is not very urgent.

Iron

The Far East is especially poor in iron ore, having only 3.2 per cent of the known reserves of the world. About one-fourth of this meagre supply is found in Manchuria and the ore is very poor in net content. Considering the size of Manchuria and its increasing industrial needs, it not only has no iron to spare, but will soon have to import iron and steel from outside. Herbert Feis in "Europe: The World's Banker," comments, "Manchuria remains, of course, primarily a buyer rather than a producer of iron and steel." Young observes that "with probable further industrialization in China, there is apparently no more iron than is necessary for her own use."

Being an agricultural country, China buys large quantities of manufactured goods from other countries, including Japan, and sells her surplus agricultural products. This form of exchange or international trade is of mutual benefit.

The Japanese claim that they must insure a steady flow of raw materials from Manchuria which are essential to their agriculture and industry. They have not been able to produce any evidence to prove that that steady flow has been threatened. At times, depreciation of Chinese currency has temporarily raised the prices. The powerful Japanese buying and shipping syndicates, such as the South Manchuria Railway Company, the Mitsui Bussan Kaisha, and the Yokohama Specie Bank, usually manage to win out in controlling the currency and the prices, though once or twice the late Chang Tso-lin almost broke the Japanese control.

The point is, therefore, not that Japan needs the raw materials of Manchuria, but how she shall secure what she needs from another country.

As far as agricultural products are concerned Manchuria will be increasingly an exporter. If the industrial development of Manchuria is to be considered, Manchuria cannot afford to export much iron and coal. Nevertheless, Japan has been exploiting the iron and coal mines exclusively for her own benefit. At the present rate of Japanese consumption, according to the expert opinion of Boris P. Torgasheff, the iron reserves in South Manchuria will be near exhaustion in ten years and coal reserves in 30 years, and the economic development of Manchuria and China will be seriously menaced. To avoid a life and death struggle for these essentials of industry, China's requirements should be considered along the side of those of Japan, and also and not the least, the requirements of Manchuria itself.

Need does not justify robbery either in private law or in international law. W. W. Willoughby, Professor at Johns Hopkins University, in the North American Review of August 1923, writes:

In the first place it may be said that the misfortunes or needs of one State give to it no ethical or moral right to violate the rights of another State, any more than they justify in private law, the seizure of one individual of another individual's property.

It is universally recognized that a country has the first claim upon the natural resources of its own soil, and may rightfully exploit or conserve them in accordance with the economic needs of its own people, whose needs rightfully take precedence over the needs of other people.

C. Walter Young, in "Japan's Special Position in Manchuria," writes:

But the 'doctrine' asserted by Japanese publicists that a State, which is manifestly poor in the gifts of nature, has a right, moral or legal, to require a comparatively richer but politically weaker State to provide for the uninterrupted flow of such resources to the needy State, is quite without parallel. . . .

Consequently, it is quite evident that in so far as this new doctrine presumes to be grounded upon any international legal validity, it is not only not supportable by international law, but contrary to one of the most universally accepted principles of that body of international rules and principles.

CHAPTER VIII

OUTSTANDING DISPUTES

Over Railways

In Chapters III and IV we have dealt with how Japan has placed obstacles in the way of the international development of Manchuria. She has also been strenuously attempting to prevent China from developing a railway system in her own territory. On the one hand, Japan has insisted upon her right to priority of investments whenever China has attempted to borrow money from abroad to build railways. China would not object to Japanese loans if long experience had not proved that to borrow money from Japan for railway building is not simply a business proposition. Japan has invariably sought to attach political strings to her railway loans. On the other hand, whenever China has tried to build railways with her own capital, Japan has made protests and threats on the ground that they may take traffic away from her railways or that they violate the "Secret Protocol of 1905." Non-official means of obstruction have also been employed. For instance, in 1927 the South Manchuria Railway Company refused to transport rails which the Chinese Government purchased from the United States, declaring that railway materials should be purchased exclusively from Japan.

China's attempt to build a railway system of her own has had a most difficult and stormy history. In some cases China has had to borrow money from Japan; in other cases, China has had to change the routes because Japan objected to their strategic character and their being parallel to her railways; and, in some cases, China has been compelled to abandon the projected lines altogether. Up to the recent Japanese occupation, China owned about 1,800 miles of railway, about one-third of which were built with Japanese loans. The objectives of the Chinese system are,

1. To connect the three provinces of Manchuria for administrative purposes;
2. To develop the economic resources within her own territory;
3. To connect her transportation system overland to a suitable harbor of her own (Hulutao).

The aims of Japan in railway building are,

1. All Chinese lines to become feeders to, and not independent of, the Japanese railways;
2. To connect Manchuria and Inner Mongolia with Korea for strategic purposes;
3. All lines to converge upon Port Arthur and Dairen which Japan controls, and China not to be permitted to develop Hulutao into a seaport of her own;
4. The tenure of all railway and port leases to be extended 99 years.

Disputes over railway building in Manchuria center around one fundamental question—Is Japan to monopolize all railway building at important economic and strategic centers or is China to be permitted to have a transportation system in her own territory in order that she may develop her own resources?

Manchuria is twice as thickly populated as is the United States, and its mileage of railways per square mile is one-seventh of the United States. So there is ample room for more railways in Manchuria. In his recent study of economic developments in Manchuria, Grover Clark of the United States wrote, "Within the last couple of years the attitude of the more liberal-minded Japanese increasingly has been that there is plenty of business in Manchuria for both the South Manchuria Railway and the Chinese lines."

Over Land Leases

Korea is a continuous part of the Asiatic Continent, adjoining Manchuria on the east. For centuries Korea had been under the suzerainty of China. Therefore, there had always been a small number of Koreans who migrated to Manchuria each year. During and after the Korean Revolution in 1920, the Korean population in Manchuria has increased by leaps and bounds. Most of them have settled in four districts in the southeastern part of Manchuria. A large number of Koreans have adopted Chinese citizenship and have settled down permanently as Chinese citizens. Most of the new-comers since 1920 are revolutionaries who are hostile towards Japan, while some of them are opportunists. The last group has made it their practice to exploit their dual citizenship. Toward the Chinese authorities they claim exterritorial rights as Japanese subjects. When they get into trouble with the Japanese authorities, they hide behind their Chinese citizenship.

The Japanese authorities in South Manchuria maintain

that where there are large numbers of Koreans, whether they be Chinese citizens or not, the Japanese must establish police stations and maintain consular jurisdiction to protect them. In the four districts where there are a large number of Koreans, there are no less than eighteen Japanese police stations that exercise the power of local government. These police stations are located outside the Japanese Leased Territory and the railway "zone," and have no treaty basis and authorization.

This "right" to police Koreans in Chinese territory has been strenuously denied by the Chinese. The reason is plain. As more Koreans come in and spread to other parts of Manchuria, it means that Japan will police the whole country. China has asked Japan to abolish these police stations, but without success. Consequently, the Chinese government has had to adopt strict regulations regarding their citizenship and their entry into Manchuria. Because of this, Japan charges the Chinese Government with inhumanity and actually shed crocodile tears over the plight of the homeless and landless Koreans denied a living in Manchuria, as if China were responsible for depriving them of their country.

Among the Twenty-One Demands that Japan presented to China in 1915, there was one condition which provided that

Japanese subjects in South Manchuria shall be granted the privilege of leasing land necessary for the erection of buildings, for commercial and industrial purposes, or for agricultural development.

Japan has been exercising this right, which seems quite

innocent if the usual interpretation of free-will leases is applied. But the Japanese interpretation of the term "lease" is (1), it means a term of at least thirty years; and (2), it is unconditionally renewable.

In this way the provision assumes immediately a sinister aspect, for land once leased will be gone forever. Moreover, land leased by Japanese subjects comes automatically under Japanese jurisdiction. The practice of the Korean opportunists and the Japanese authorities has caused clashes and disputes between the Chinese and the Koreans, as well as between the Chinese and Japanese authorities. On the one hand, the Japanese want to extend their jurisdiction as widely as possible, while, on the other hand, the Chinese have been apprehensive that in leasing and selling land to Japanese subjects, they are enlarging the Japanese sphere of influence.

Grover Clark believes that "this leasing right, if conceded, moreover, would hold for all nationals in all parts of China under the 'most favored nation' clauses. It would thus break down one of China's most valuable means of protection—the confinement of the foreign commercial properties to the treaty ports." Other authorities point out that the fact that the other powers have not claimed the same "rights" demanded by Japan in the Twenty-One Demands under the "most favored nation" clauses, implies that they have not recognized the validity of those "rights" and of the "1915 Agreements."

Railway Settlements and Railway Guards

After the Russo-Japanese War, as a temporary emergency measure, Japan maintained railway guards. But, in the additional agreements to the Sino-Japanese treaty of December 22, 1905, Japan pledged the following:

ART. II.—In view of the earnest desire expressed by the Imperial Chinese Government to have the Japanese and Russian troops and railway guards in Manchuria withdrawn as soon as possible, and in order to meet this desire, the Imperial Japanese Government, in the event of Russia agreeing to the withdrawal of her railway guards, or in case other proper measures are agreed to between China and Russia, consent to take similar steps accordingly. . . .

Russian troops have been withdrawn long since while Japanese railway guards have remained and Japan has refused to withdraw them though repeatedly requested so to do by the Chinese Government. Moreover, these railway guards are not what would be ordinarily considered guards. They are regular troops with war equipment which Japan can use at any time to bring military pressure to bear upon Chinese authorities.

Japan has delayed the withdrawal of railway guards for over a quarter of a century on the ground that conditions have not yet become normal and peaceful. Of course she defines normal and peaceful conditions to suit her own purposes. C. Walter Young in his book on "Japanese Jurisdiction in the South Manchuria Railway Area," writes:

Consequently, when Japan acquired the transfer at Portsmouth of that portion of the Chinese Eastern Railway south of Kuanchengtzu, there was no agreement between Russia and China as to the extent of the Russian rights within that area. Japan received, therefore, from Russia a questionable right to exercise unlimited administrative authority within the various municipalities, or 'Railway towns,' strung along that portion of the Chinese Eastern which, after 1906, became the South Manchuria Railway. . . .

The conclusion would seem to be that this grant of 'the absolute and exclusive right of administration of its lands' to the railway company, i.e., to the Russian management, warranted the establishment on the part of the company of some form of political control over such lands as were actually necessary for the company to use for its establishment as a transportation system. As to just what form of political authority may reasonably be assumed there is room for question. Evidently not the right to levy taxes anywhere, nor the right to establish courts of law. The latter was specifically reserved to the Chinese local authorities . . . the railway 'settlements' was the principal object of the Chinese official protests, and of continual friction with the local authorities, it is noteworthy that no such special institution was provided for in the railway agreements with China. As for stationing of regular troops along the railway, that was specifically prohibited in both the treaty of alliance and the railway agreement of 1896.

In the *Appeal from the Chinese Government Under Article XV of the Covenant* to the League of Nations dated February 29, 1932, the Chinese Government stated:

Railway guards were kept by Japan along the railways after the Russo-Japanese War originally on the ground of the post bellum disorder in Manchuria, but have been maintained there ever since against Chinese protests. They consist of the following kinds:

(a) One division of regular troops, with headquarters at Liaoyang and garrison points at Changchun, Kungtsuling, Tiehling, Mukden, Liaoyang and Haicheng, besides Port Arthur in the Leased Territory; and

(b) Six battalions of specially organized guards stationed along the railways, with headquarters at Kungtsuling.

The railway guards are under the control of the Commander of the Kwantung Army, with headquarters in the Leased Territory, who, according to the Japanese Imperial Ordinance of April 12th, 1919, is to "have command over the military forces in the Kwantung Province and South Manchuria"; to "be responsible for the defence of the Kwantung Province and the protection of the railway lines in South Manchuria"; and to "have the power to employ military forces" in discharging his duties, "when he deems it necessary." The article containing the last provision continues:

> The Commander shall comply with the request of the Governor of Kwantung for the despatch of troops necessary for the preservation of peace and order in the region under the Governor's jurisdiction, as well as in connection with police affairs in the lands attached to the South Manchuria Railway; but he may adopt such expedient military measure as occasion may require in case of emergency too urgent to wait for a request from the Governor.
>
> Any such contingencies as the foregoing shall be reported to the Minister of War and the Chief of the General Staff.

With regard to railway guards, the claim that they have a treaty basis of their own cannot be any better sustained. Article V of the Chinese Eastern Railway contract reads:

> The Chinese Government will take measures to assure the safety of the railway and of the persons in its service against any attack.
>
> The Company will have the right to employ at will as many foreigners or natives as it may find necessary for the purpose of administration, etc.
>
> Criminal cases, lawsuits, etc., upon the territory of the railway, must be settled by the local authorities in accordance with the stipulations of the Treaties.

The foregoing translation from the French text may also be compared with a translation from the Chinese text, which reads:

> The said railway and its employées the Chinese Government will take measures to protect. As to the personnel, Chinese and foreign, necessary for the operation of the railway, the said Company is permitted to employ at will. All criminal cases, lawsuits, etc., upon the lands of the railway shall be administered by the local authorities in accordance with Treaties.

It is clear from the foregoing provisions that Japan did not have a right to maintain railway guards.

That such is the case is, it may be added, recognized by Japan herself. In Additional Article I in the Portsmouth Treaty, Japan reserves with Russia "the right to maintain guards to protect their respective railway lines in Manchuria," the number of such "not to exceed fifteen per kilometre." In Additional Article II in the Peking Treaty of 1905, under the protest of China, she, however, not only makes no claim to a "right," but undertakes to withdraw the guards under certain conditions. This Article, translated from the Chinese text, reads:

> Since the Chinese Government declares that it earnestly hopes that Japan and Russia will rapidly withdraw their troops now in Manchuria as well as the railway guards, the Japanese Government is prepared to meet China's wishes. When Russia agrees to withdraw her railway guards, or when China and Russia agree to adopt other proper measures, the Japanese Government will consent to take similar steps. Again, when the order of Manchuria is restored and China is in the position to give full protection to the lives and property of foreigners, Japan will also simultaneously with Russia withdraw the railway guards.

Since Japan has no right to maintain the guards and has so admitted, their withdrawal is but a matter of duty. It may also be added that, even on the basis of the two alternative conditions she imposed for carrying out her duty, she has no reason to tarry. "When Russia agrees," runs the first condition, "to withdraw her railway guards, or when China and Russia agree to adopt other proper measures, the Japanese Government will consent to take similar steps." It is a common knowledge that Russia has so agreed. "The Governments of the Contracting Parties," says Article IX, Section I, of the Sino-Russian Pekin Agreement of May 31st, 1924, "declare that, with the exception of matters pertaining to the business operations which are under the direct control of the Chinese Eastern Railway, all other matters affecting the right of the National and Local Governments of the Republic of China, such as . . . matters relating to . . . military administration . . . shall be administered by the Chinese authorities." "When the order of Manchuria is restored," runs the alternative Japanese condition, "and China is in the position to give full protection to the lives and property of foreigners, Japan will also, simultaneously with Russia, withdraw the railway guards." It is scarcely necessary to say that the restoration to a normal, from a post bellum, situation, which is contemplated in the text and is the only condition that could have been contemplated there, must have taken place not long after the cessation of armed conflict between Japan and Russia. At least, there has been no indication to the contrary ever since the reorganization of the Manchurian administration in 1907, from which time twenty-five years have now elapsed.

CHAPTER IX

"TREATY RIGHTS" AND "TREATY VIOLATIONS," ETC.

JAPAN has always insisted on interpreting treaties in her own way and when there has been any doubt or dispute she has always refused to arbitrate, but has proceeded to carry out her own interpretations. For instance, she has refused to have the validity and equity of the following two treaties adjudicated by an international tribunal: The "1915 Agreements" resulted from the Twenty-One Demands, and the "1905 Secret Protocol" on parallel railway lines. About the extension of her jurisdiction over Chinese territory and the maintenance of troops along the railways she has invariably refused a neutral interpretation of the exact meaning of the original agreements.

Japan Utilizes Corrupt Local Officials

In order to strengthen her special position, she has made it a practice to influence and intimidate local officials (who have had no authority to sign treaties) to make secret agreements that will furnish her pretexts to make further inroads upon China's sovereignty. Consequently, no one knows how many of these so-called secret "treaties" are in existence which have not the slightest legality. As C. Walter Young wrote:

55

The rancoring rebuffs which local Chinese officials have suffered at the hands of Japanese soldiers, police and consular officials throughout the South Manchuria Railway area, and the questionable assumption of jurisdiction by Japanese officials in native villages adjoining the Japanese railway towns, have been matched on the Chinese side by their own confused system of local government, the incompetence of local officials in municipal administration, and the occasional ignorance and irregular practices—including acceptance of bribes and "squeese"—of the local Chinese officials.

On some of Japan's "Treaty rights" he quoted Lo Wenkan, now the Foreign Minister of China:

The important fact to consider with regard to the rights exercised by the Japanese in the South Manchuria Railway areas is that these rights have been required more by usage than by specific grant in bilateral treaties or agreements between China and Japan. The Japanese have acted on the assumption that, because the Russians exercised certain administrative functions in the Chinese Eastern Railway areas before 1905, Japan acquired similar rights along the South Manchuria Railway by virtue of the Treaty of Portsmouth. This contention is tenable only to the degree to which China actually sanctioned the exercise of administrative rights by the Russians, and to the degree to which these presumed rights have been recognized by usage, usage which may establish a legal right in fact. That China questioned the exercise of administrative authority by the Russians in the Chinese Eastern Railway areas was evident before 1905, but more evident after the question of the Harbin municipality arose in 1908.

There is today, however, a situation which complicates the whole question of the Japanese rights. Very probably secret agreements were negotiated by the late Marshal Chang Tso-lin's government at Mukden with the Japanese authorities, agreements which the Chinese officials, who negotiated them, have for personal reasons kept secret, even from the Foreign Intercourse Office at Mukden. I myself had occasion to come across a great many irregular settlements which the Chinese made through Mukden of questions which gave the

Japanese special rights in certain land cases which were never sanctioned by any of the treaties.

The Chinese local authorities, especially under the government of the late Marshal Chang Tso-lin, were inclined to settle such cases especially when hard pressed by the Japanese for settlement, without much regard to whether or not the treaties sanctioned such action, and as a natural result of the Chinese characteristic of careless disregard for the formalities of treaties and of the desire to settle individual cases on their own merits, or to avoid friction. Consequently, the records of the Foreign Intercourse Office in Mukden are incomplete and scattered. It is almost impossible to ascertain exactly what rights have been sacrificed in one way or another by these irregular settlements without the sanction of the Peking Government. (Quoted in "Japanese Jurisdiction in the South Manchuria Railway Areas.")

The Famous Koga Case

Japanese publicists have tried to create the impression that China has a monopoly on official corruption, which impression Japan has utilized to her advantage, and which she has also capitalized to condone her own actions in Manchuria. Mr. A. Moran Young, British editor of the Japan *Chronicle* (published in Japan), writes in "Japan in Recent Times," a book which describes the inside of Japanese politics:

The ramifications of the case were extraordinary and preliminary examinations lasted over a year, during which time it was found advisable to dismiss Dr. Koga from his post of Director of the Colonization Bureau and to search the house of Koga's associates, including the Marquis Inoue. The names of distinguished men were involved in the scandal. Procurator-General Hiranuma, long before the preliminary examination was finished, ascribed the whole disgraceful business to the degeneracy of the upper classes. All kinds of corruption were disclosed. The South Manchuria Railway in one case bought a coal mine from a member of the Diet (of the Government party, naturally) at a very high price. Enormous sums were paid for the privilege of selling opium to the Chinese. Brokers interested in the creation of an Exchange at Dairen facilitated the process with a gift of 100,000 *yen*. Every sort of bribery and graft seemed to centre around the Kwantung and S.M.R. administration, and the farther the inquiry went the more deeply was the Tokyo Government itself implicated. It was the first government really based on a political party—the Seiyukai—and the party had to obtain funds. Some of the evidence pointed to the Dairen Opium Bureau being its principal means of support.

Japan prohibits with severe penalties her own subjects to use opium, but she has never seriously attempted to restrict the sale of opium in her leased territories in China. The League of Nations' Commission of Enquiry reported in 1931 that the net revenue in the Japanese leased territory and the South Manchuria Railway "zone" derived from the Japanese Bureau of Opium Monopoly amounted to 20,015,196 *yen*.

Security of Japanese Nationals

The Japanese nationals in China have been much safer than have been the Chinese nationals in Japan. The total number of Japanese civilians killed in all of "chaotic" China during the last ten years up to the recent invasion is less than half the number of Chinese civilians massacred in "well govrened" Korea last summer directly under the eyes of the Japanese military and police authorities. Even after Japanese forces occupied Manchuria and bombed and killed civilians at Mukden, Chinchow and other cities, the Chinese people maintained self-control in spite of the high feeling aroused. Mrs. F. Louis Slade, prominent American citizen and delegate to the Conference of the Institute of Pacific Relations, said, in a public address in New York City on March 10, 1932, "From September 18th to November 20th when I left China, no Japanese subjects were disturbed in all of China, excepting one incident which occurred in Hongkong. It was remarkable, in spite of the great provocation, how safe the Japanese had been. If a similar invasion happened to us, spontaneous retaliations would have been terrible."

Usually clashes between Japanese and Chinese are due to the arrogance of the former. The fact that recently Japanese soldiers and civilians had the audacity to beat up American consular officials in Mukden and Shanghai without provocation shows forcibly the greater arrogance and injustice with which they are in the habit of dealing with the Chinese whom they consider a conquered people. Stanley K. Hornbeck writes in "Contemporary Politics in the Far East,"

This penetration of the Interior, and the unauthorized opening of shops in remote towns by these commercial pioneers has been a matter of annoyance to the Chinese officials, especially on account of the numerous conflicts with the local Chinese and consequent controversies with the Japanese officials to which the practice gives rise. The Manchuria Daily News prints every little while accounts of such conflicts, the blame always being laid upon the Chinese.

One of the chief causes for complaints made against Japanese methods both by the foreigners who live in Manchuria and by the Chinese, and perhaps foremost among the causes of personal clash and official controversy, has been the officiousness and brutality of the police and soldiers. The Japanese have full administrative control, including exclusive police jurisdiction, within the Railway zone; at

the same time they frequently and without hesitation encroach upon
Chinese rights outside the zone. Thus, for instance, Japanese soldiers pass freely under arms throughout the regions adjoining the
Railway zone, while Chinese police and soldiers are only on rare
occasions and after obtaining express permission from the Japanese
allowed to enter the zone.

It is from the Japanese police, however, and from Chinese detec-
tives in their employ, that trouble usually comes. A huge list could
be made of instances which have been reported during the past ten
years, and it is well known that a great many instances never attain
publicity. The notorious incident which occurred at Changli, just
outside of Manchuria and on undisputed Chinese soil, in September
1913, was reported beyond the confines of the Far East. Here, as a
result of a quarrel between a soldier of the Japanese railway guard
and a Chinese fruit-vender, the former refusing to pay the latter for
wares he was consuming, Japanese guards set upon and killed five
Chinese policemen. The investigation which followed showed that
the Japanese were clearly the aggressor and had acted with wanton
brutality.

Chinese "Provocations"

During the last quarter of a century, Japan has accomplished in South Manchuria the following:

1. Secured the control of railways and leaseholds in South Manchuria by war with Russia.

2. Extended the terms of control of the same from 25 to 99 years
through the presentation of the Twenty-One Demands in 1915.

3. Remained in control of the railways and leaseholds after the
original terms expired in 1923.

4. Enforced her "treaty rights" according to her own interpretations.

5. Established economic control and railway monopoly.

6. Extended her political domination and jurisdiction over Chinese territory.

7. Interfered in China's domestic affairs.

What could China do in the face of such an aggressive military power bent on eventually swallowing up Manchuria as she did Korea? On one hand, she has not yet developed an army and navy strong enough to oust the aggressor, and, on the other hand, Japan has always used military pressure in direct negotiation and refused the settlement of disputes by international arbitration or adjudication.

A burglar is attempting to strangle a sick man who struggles and hits back, although very feebly. Of course, if the sick man yielded, all would be peaceful and pleasing to the robber. The tactics of the sick man may be characterized as "provoking," depending upon the premise you begin with and how you look at it.

The same applies to the alleged "54" or "300" cases of violations of Japan's "scores of treaties" in Manchuria from the Japanese point of view. After the burglar has beaten the owner of the house and occupied part of his home, could the burglar expect the owner to treat him courteously and scrupulously, as if he were a legitimate tenant? The numerously alleged "violations" could be summarized as one great "violation," that is, China has not bowed to every wish of Japan and yielded gently to her every act of aggression and exploitation. All Japan's "treaty rights" since 1915 may be said to have been conceived in iniquity and born of imperialism.

CHAPTER X

THE FINAL RECKONING

Japan's Positive Policy

JAPAN's victories over China and Russia awakened in her the dream of world conquest. As early as 1905 the political leaders of Japan, especially Komura and Hayashi, formulated the Greater Japan policy, which consisted of the following four steps:

1. Expansion on the Asiatic continent.
2. Seizure of Manchuria.
3. Subordination of China.
4. Friendship of Russia.

Among the secret documents of the Czarist régime published by Soviet Russia, there were revealed two secret treaties concluded between Russia and Japan in 1907 and 1909 for the partition of China, with specific reference to Manchuria and Inner Mongolia. A complete account of those agreements is found in V. A. Yakhontoff's book, "Russia and the Soviet Union in the Far East."

The Japanese imperialists saw that, in order to dominate the Pacific area, Japan must have sufficient raw materials and a base for military operations on the Asiatic continent. Manchuria has proved to be the territory from which China could be dominated. Its strategic value is greatly enhanced by the fact that it contains rich natural resources. How could Japan expect to seize Manchuria without the opposition of China?

Therefore, Japan must keep China weak, and the most effective way to keep a large country like China weak is to keep her divided. The aim of Japan's Positive Policy toward China during the last quarter of a century has been to keep her weak and divided so that Japan could seize Manchuria in order to realize a "Greater Japan." O course, the Japanese government has denied, and will continue to deny, that Japan has any imperialistic designs, but actions speak louder than words. The true intentions of Japan, especially of the military clique which dominates the Japanese government, have been made as plain as daylight by her series of aggressions on China since 1905.

Recent Evidences of the Positive Policy

The so-called Manchurian war lord, Chang Tso-lin, to whom Japan points as an example of Chinese official corruption, had been a puppet of the Japanese government. His rise to that dominant position was due to Japanese support, which began after the Russo-Japanese War, during which Chang fought on the Japanese side. In 1925 when Kuo Sung-ling threatened to eliminate Chang Tso-lin, Japan came to his assistance. After Kuo was defeated, Chang Tso-lin publicly thanked Japan for her assistance. Unfortunately for Chang, he later dared to disobey Japan's wishes and began to develop a Chinese railway system in

Manchuria. In June, 1928, when his train was passing under the Japanese guarded railway bridge of the South Manchuria Railway a bomb set by expert hands removed Chang as an obstacle to Japan's ambitions.

In the same year, there was a good opportunity for the Nationalist army to unify China. On the wave of popular support, the Nationalist Party had been able to advance rapidly from Canton to Hankow and Nanking. When the Nationalist army was advancing through Shantung towards Tientsin, Japan intervened and blocked its advance, and provoked a fight with the Nationalist army at Tsinan. The Tsinan affair of May 3, 1928, was thus added to the long series of Japan's interventions by force. According to the findings of the Chinese Government the damages caused by the Japanese troops at Tsinan were as follows:

Chinese civilians and soldiers killed	1,700
Value of public property destroyed	$11,300,000
Value of private property destroyed	21,800,000

Chang Hsueh-liang, the son of Chang Tso-lin, was planning to join the newly established Nationalist Government at Nanking. The Japanese Government immediately sent a special envoy to warn Chang Hsueh-liang not to hoist the Nationalist flag, nor to unite with the rest of China. Young Chang hesitated for six months, but finally decided to throw his lot with the rest of China. Japan never forgave him for his disobedience. General Honjo, Commander of the Japanese forces in the recent invasion, openly declared in September, 1931, that one of his aims was to oust Chang Hsueh-liang from Manchuria. When he captured Mukden he packed Chang's personal belongings in 437 cases and shipped them to the deposed governor of Manchuria with a note in a sarcastic vein, reminding him that Japan had warned him before and that now it was too late for him to think of returning to his capital!

This Policy has accomplished a twofold purpose for Japan: (1), she has prevented the setting up of a strong and effective Chinese government in Manchuria; and (2), she has used the lack of a strong Chinese government as a pretext to seize Manchuria.

Nationalism vs. Anti-Foreignism

The seemingly unchanging China has been changing, and rapidly, during recent years. China has awakened. She instinctively thinks first of self-preservation. She discovers Nationalism, the secret of power of a modern nation, and the modern definition of sovereign rights. What the modern powers would defend to the last man, has been taken away from China by those very powers. The unequal treaties they imposed upon China almost a century ago, have worked great injustices. In spite of the fact that conditions have changed and New China's aspirations are legitimate, the powers, especially Japan, have been unwilling to remove those unjust conditions so as to provide the fullest opportunity for China to work out her own problems. The Chinese people could no longer ignore or keep silent about those unequal and unjust treaties. Call it anti-foreignism, if you wish; it is anti-foreign injustices. In this sense, the Thirteen Colonies of America were also "anti-foreign."

The Nationalist Movement of China is based on the Three People's Principles:

1. The people shall all have a fair livelihood.
2. The people shall all have a voice in the government.
3. The Chinese people shall rule China themselves.

A united and strong Nationalist China would put an end to foreign aggression and exploitation. When China recovers all her sovereign rights, Japan will lose the special position she has usurped in Manchuria. She has foreseen the approach of the day of final reckoning. Either she will have to adopt the policy of conciliation so that the fundamental interests of the two countries in Manchuria will be readjusted on the basis of to live and let live, or she must strike before New China becomes of age.

PART TWO

THE CRISIS

CHAPTER XI

THE IMMEDIATE CAUSES

The Bomb of September 18

THE bomb of September 18, 1931, set off a chain of events without parallel in modern history. The undeclared war that followed has surpassed conventional wars in ferocity and bitterness. The League of Nations had to convene special meetings of the Council and the Assembly, and for the first time the League Council voted 13 to 1 on an important question. Breaking all precedents, the United States cooperated with the League in appointing a representative to sit with the Council, and in officially declaring more than once that it approved of the steps taken by the League. Representatives of great powers have publicly admitted that the crisis challenges the very foundation of the world's peace machinery.

Mr. Chester H. Rowell, well-known American publicist and Information Secretary of the American Council of the Institute of Pacific Relations, was in Mukden at the time of the outbreak in September. He reports the incident as follows:

By a coincidence as remarkable as that of the earlier bombing of Chang Tso-lin, it did happen at 10.30 on the night of September 18. The story of that night has already been told a hundred times (and ways), but it may not be generally realized that the "destruction" of the railway near Mukden, resulting in the stupendous Japanese action of "self-defense" that has been going on ever since, consisting of cracking the fishplate at the junction of two rails, damaging the rail flange for two feet each side of the junction, and knocking a few splinters off a wooden sleeper. Who actually set the bomb may never be known and it is not, after all, important. The attack on the railway line may have happened exactly as the Japanese tell it. The significant point is that on its alleged happening, the Japanese based certain actions.

As an honest reporter, however, I must record that, besides being myself unable to accept the Japanese version of the story after seeing and hearing the evidence on the ground, I interviewed every other neutral observer I could find, journalistic or military, in a position to form an opinion and not one of them believed it either. (Published in Asia, April, 1932).

Agitation by Japanese Army

Early in September the army officers of Japan were agitating for strong action in China, calling upon the Japanese people to support them in the seizure of Manchuria. Hugh Byas in a special cable to the New York *Times* on September 9, 1931, reported from Japan,

Tokyo Planes Fan Hatred of Mukden

How the Nakamura case—the slaying of Captain Shintaro Nakamura in Manchuria last month—is inflaming sentiment regarding Japan's Manchurian problems is shown by the astonishing action of a squadron of six army airplanes.

These planes, in a recent practice flight around the Japanese Alps, dropped leaflets reported to number 100,000, calling on the nation to awaken to the dangers menacing Japanese rights in Manchuria.

Kanazawa was flooded with the pamphlets, which are striking in appearance and vigorous in content. Printed in red, white and black, they show a stealthy clawlike hand, typifying China, extended over the Japanese flag, on which is printed an itemized list of the thirteen Japanese rights in Manchuria.

Above the flag is a slogan, "Fellow Countrymen, Awaken for National Defense!" Beneath is an outline map of Manchuria, with three lines reading:

The cost of the Russo-Japanese War was 2,000,000 yen.
Japanese investments in Manchuria total 1,700,000 yen.
Our countrymen who died numbered 200,000.

The Nakamura Case

Sometime toward the end of June, 1931, Captain Nakamura of Japan disappeared with three companions while travelling in Western Manchuria and Inner Mongolia. What actually happened to Nakamura and his group will probably never be known, but some significant details have been ascertained. In the first place, it has been proved that Captain Nakamura was on active duty as an officer of the Japanese army when he went into Inner Mongolia. Instead of making known his identity to the Chinese authorities, he held a falsified passport, disguising himself as a teacher of geography. It is also certain that he and his companions were making maps and photographs of military importance. The Japanese government alleges that Chinese troops shot Nakamura and his companions as spies.

Riots in Manchuria and Korea

In July there occurred in Wanpaoshan a clash between Chinese and Korean farmers. The latter group dug a canal through land owned by the Chinese farmers who attempted to fill up the canal. Japanese police took part in the clash and started firing. The incident was not serious as there were no casualties, but the Japanese controlled press used it to fan the hatred of the Koreans in Korea whose retaliation resulted in serious anti-Chinese riots in Korea. These riots lasted seven days resulting in the massacre of 148 and the wounding of twice as many defenseless Chinese men, women, and children, and hundreds of homes were destroyed. The total number of Koreans and Japanese civilians in all "chaotic" China who had lost their lives during the last ten years up to the invasion is less than half the number of Chinese people massacred in "well-governed" Korea in July, 1931, right under the eyes of Japanese military and police authorities.

The comparison is more striking when it is remembered that in China there are over 1,000,000 Japanese and Koreans scattered all over the country, while there are but a few thousand Chinese people concentrated in a few cities in Korea.

The Japan Chronicle commented upon the riots in Korea, on July 9, 1931, as follows:

The Chinese residents of Heijo subject to a reign of terror and the authorities scarcely lifted a finger to help them . . .

If the sword had been in the other hand there would have been a nation-wide outcry. The murder of a Japanese is always good material for the interventionists to broadcast as solid proof of the fact that China cannot guarantee safety of life and property.

Up to August, Japan had not even accepted responsibility for the anti-Chinese riots in Korea, while China had already promised to investigate and negotiate for the settlement of the Nakamura and Wanpaoshan cases. The Chinese government had already ordered the arrest of the Commander of the Chinese garrison in Inner Mongolia and promised proper punishment if it should be proved that the Chinese garrison had anything to do with the disappearance of Captain Nakamura.

According to a special cable to the New York *Times,* dated August 9, 1931, it was reported:

> The Japanese press still displays excitement over the slaying of Captain Nakamura in Manchuria on August 17, but the Foreign Office does not expect any developments for a week or ten days, when new investigators sent out by the Civil Governor of Mukden return.

> .   .   .   .

> In the meantime, General Ying, the Mukden Chief of Staff, has been summoned to Peiping for a conference with Marshal Chang Hsueh-liang, Commander of the Manchurian Third Army, whose soldiers have been accused of killing the Japanese.

China Willing to Arbitrate

The Japanese Government refused to wait for the result of the investigation to ascertain the true causes of the disappearance of Nakamura and his companions, but insisted that China should accept all the Japanese claims in this case, the Wanpaoshan case, and all questions regarding Japanese land and railway rights in Manchuria. As early as the beginning of September, the Japanese Government had already intimated to the head of the Government of Manchuria, Chang Hsueh-liang, that Japan would take effective measures if he did not accept the claims of the Japanese Government. It was at this juncture that the representatives of Chang Hsueh-liang issued a statement suggesting that the League of Nations attempt to settle all the disputes between China and Japan. "We strongly favor having the League of Nations appoint a representative to live in Manchuria and exhaustively investigate all phases of Sino-Japanese controversies." (Special cable to the New York *Times* by Hallett Abend, September 3, 1931.)

It thus became clear that Japan would not consent to settle her disputes by arbitration but intended to impose her wishes upon China by force. Early in September General Honjo, a veteran officer of the Japanese army and a strong supporter of the Positive Policy, was made Commander of Japanese forces in Manchuria. In the meantime, four army divisions and two naval units were ordered to mobilize on a war basis. Chang Hsueh-liang apparently anticipated some form of military action by Japan, although he did not fully realize the seriousness of the situation. Early in September he issued a secret order to the officers in his army and to the Commissioners of Police in Manchuria to the effect that, in case of attack, the Chinese troops and police were not to resist.

Cesare in *Outlook and Independent*
The Open Door

CHAPTER XII

THE MILITARY OCCUPATION

Japanese Attack Premeditated

ALL neutral observers and eye-witnesses agree that the Japanese attack in Manchuria was premeditated and unprovoked.

Upton Close, an American writer and eye-witness, by wireless to the New York *Times,* on October 11, 1931, stated:

> Foreigners in Mukden agree that the Japanese attack was premeditated and unprovoked and carried out with extreme ruthlessness for the purpose of striking terror among Chinese forces everywhere.

Dr. Sherwood Eddy, veteran American Y. M. C. A. worker and an eye-witness, in a cable published in the New York *Herald Tribune* on October 14, 1931, stated:

> I was present at the capture of Mukden. Evidence of many witnesses interviewed at time and on spot points to premeditated carefully prepared offensive plan of Japanese army without provocation of any Chinese attack, producing bitter resentment when Chinese suffering with flood disaster and world preoccupied. Japanese troops not withdrawn, but all strategic points bombed. I testify to evidence of efforts to establish puppet independent government in Manchuria under Japanese military control. I have forwarded sworn statements of interviews with Chinese leaders in Manchuria who testify to repeated

75

pressure of Japanese to induce them to head independent governments.

Extent of Military Occupation

In spite of protests by the members of the League of Nations and the United States, Japanese forces have advanced further and further into Chinese territory. Since September the Japanese military occupation has extended to Tsitsihar and Harbin on the north, the Great Wall on the south, Inner Mongolia and Jehol on the west, and the Korean border on the east—an area of over 200,000 square miles, twice the area of New England and the New York State combined.

In this occupied area Chinese troops and police who had been ordered not to resist, have been disarmed. Chinese schools, banks and private businesses have been taken over or closed; Chinese administrative organs have been completely destroyed; numerous Chinese officials and private citizens have been arrested and put to death; and a great deal of Chinese property has been destroyed. In this wide area, which constitutes over two-thirds of Manchuria and in which 97 per cent of the people are Chinese, Japan has set up her own political administration and rules the territory through her own puppets who are nominally the officials of the "independent" government, and the Japanese have taken over as well private businesses and industries, and have set up a permanent economic structure for the exclusive control of all the resources, industries, and trade.

The Manchester *Guardian* of England published the following report on January 15, 1932:

JAPAN'S GRIP ON MANCHURIA

Complete Economic Control

(From our Correspondent in Manchuria) Mukden, December 17.

The Japanese General Staff in Tokio announced on December 6 that the Japanese army had decided to support the policy of the 'open door' in Manchuria, and that the investment of foreign capital in both Manchuria and Mongolia would be welcomed. Further, it was stated ("Japan Advertiser," December 7) that Japan would not insist upon a predominant position as regards economic rights, and that the old policy of centering all Manchurian affairs around the Japanese owned and controlled South Manchuria Railway 'would be abandoned.' While the official announcement to the foregoing effect as made in Tokio, it was asserted that the new policy was being sponsored by the Japanese army headquarters in Mukden, and that an investigation was in process of being carried out by the Japanese military authorities in Mukden regarding the establishment of the new policy pertaining to economic affairs.

In view of these statements it is of considerable significance to examine recent economic and political developments in Manchuria since the Japanese military occupation on September 18. The following information has been compiled from foreign (non-Japanese) sources, and is authoritative:

Fengtien Peace-Maintenance Committee

This committee, headed by the veteran Chinese official Yuan Chin-kai, was organized under the personal direction of the two ranking Japanese military commanders, General Honjo and Colonel Doihara, shortly following the Japanese occupation. The committee is composed of old officials, some of them dating back to the Ching Dynasty. It has three Japanese advisers, Messrs. Imagi, Naribi, and Kanboka, and, in addition, some twenty additional Japanese attaches (Secret Service men), who serve on the committee as 'protectors.'

Mukden Municipal Office

Immediately following the Japanese occupation of Mukden on September 18, when the former Chinese Administration collapsed, the Japanese army appointed Colonel Doihara as Acting Mayor of Mukden, Colonel Doihara having previously served as 'adviser' to Marshal Chang Hsueh-liang and liaison officer between the Chinese Administration and the Japanese Kwantung army, with headquarters at Port Arthur. Later the Japanese caused a Japanese-educated Chinese lawyer named Chao Ching-po to be appointed as Mayor of Mukden with Colonel Doihara as adviser. Still later Colonel Doihara was transferred to Tientsin, and, according to the Chinese authorities, he was involved in the abortive plan to restore the Manchu 'Boy Emperor' Pu-Yi to the Manchu throne in Mukden. At any rate, Colonel Doihara's place was taken by two other Japanese advisers, one named Nakano, who was appointed adviser to the municipality, and another named Okakiti, who was made special adviser to Chao Ching-po. In addition eight other Japanese were appointed supervisors to the various municipal departments, including foreign affairs office. Also, a large number of other Japanese were added to the municipal payroll as bodyguards to the Mayor and for other undesignated purposes.

Fengtien Municipal Police

Previously entirely Chinese from the standpoint of personnel and control. Now controlled entirely by the local Mukden Japanese gendarmery, which has its headquarters in the Japanese Concession.

Fengtien Bureau of Finance

Controlled by Japanese adviser named Irobe and staff of Japanese assistants.

Fengtien Bureau of Industries

This important bureau, which previously had control of the granting of concessions for industrial and commercial establishments, mining ventures, etc., is controlled by a Japanese supervisor named Hashino.

Fengtien Telegraphs

Nominally controlled by Ching Pi-tung, a Manchu who is a son of the late Prince Su. In addition, Mr. Chin is managing director of the Changchun-Kirin-Tunhwa Railway and also head of the so-called Northeastern Telegraph Administration, which previously had control of all telegraphic, telephonic, and radio communication in the three northeastern provinces. Mr. Chin was appointed to these three positions by the commander of the Japanese army in Mukden, but actual control of the Fengtien Bureau of Telegraphs is exercised by a large staff of Japanese censors who supervise all incoming and outgoing messages.

Mukden Telegraph Office

Controlled by Japanese adviser named Nagagibe.

Chinese Post Office at Mukden

The Foreign Commissioner, Mr. Frank Poletti, a technical advisory official appointed by the Central Government, in accordance with international understanding, still functions in the Mukden office along with the Chinese postal officials, but Japanese control is effected in two ways, first by two Japanese employees of the Post Office who have been authorized by General Honjo to inspect all postal accounts and reports on behalf of Japanese army headquarters. Further control is exercised through seven Japanese mail censors who have been placed in the post office by the Japanese army ostensibly for the purpose of preventing Chinese military officers and officials who were expelled from Manchuria from communicating with alleged agents in Mukden. It is asserted that the censors do not interfere with mail containing foreign addresses owing to the desire of the Japanese to avoid complications with foreigners or the foreign Consular body at Mukden. The censors have access to all mail containing Chinese addresses, and many foreign residents of Mukden allege they have evidence of their mail being tampered with.

BANKS AND BUSINESS CONCERNS

Bank of the Three Eastern Provinces

This bank, the official financial organ of the former Manchurian Government, was taken over by the Japanese military and sealed on the night of the occupation of Mukden. The Japanese commander immediately set a number of auditors to work ferreting out the financial secrets of Marshal Chang Hsueh-liang and other officials of the late Administration. Since the closure of this bank, as well as of the Frontier Bank, which was owned directly by Marshal Chang Hsueh-liang, paralyzed all business in Manchuria except that conducted through the Japanese banks, it led to strong protests by the foreign Consular authorities. Finally the Japanese permitted the Chinese banks to reopen under the supervision of a Japanese adviser. Mr. Suda, and some eight 'counselors,' who serve as heads of the various departments and whose signatures must be obtained on all important transactions.

Bank of China and Bank of Communications

These Manchurian branches of the large Chinese private banks with headquarters in Shanghai are not controlled by Japanese advisers stationed on the premises, but all important transactions are subject to the supervision of the Japanese financial adviser, Mr. Suda, who controls the two Chinese official banks.

Li-Da Company

This important Chinese company, owned by the Bank of the Three Eastern Provinces, was founded by the Chinese commercial and financial interests of Manchuria and had official backing for the purpose of competing with the powerful Japanese interests such as Mitsui and Co. It virtually controlled the export of soya-beans, wheat, and other native products, and assisted in the financing of Chinese public enterprises such as the construction of railways, opening of mines, etc. The company has now been taken over completely by the Japanese, and, according to reports of the Chinese employees, it is either to be liquidated or operated as an auxiliary of the Japanese companies.

Mukden Cotton Mill

Previously Chinese owned and operated, but after being closed for a considerable period recently reopened under Japanese supervision.

Fu-Chou-Wan Coal Company

Largest Chinese-owned coal mine in Manchuria and chief competitor of the Fushun mines, which are owned and operated by the South Manchuria Railway. Now operated directly by the Japanese.

The Chinese selling agency for the mine, which supplied much of the coal used by Chinese interests at Mukden, recently was warned that it would be closed unless it purchased at least 50 per cent of its supplies from Fushun.

Pen-Chi-Hu Coal Mine

Previously was a Sino-Japanese enterprise, but was forcibly taken over by the Japanese and all Chinese officials ousted.

Mukden Electric Light Company

Constructed and operated by the Chinese with the object of assuring independence from the Japanese electric power monopoly operated as a subsidiary of the South Manchuria Railway, the Japanese plant being located at Fushun with high-tension lines paralleling the S. M. R. tracks. The Japanese army took over the Mukden Electric Light Company on the day following the Japanese occupation, and now operate it with a Japanese manager and heads of departments. Since that time the Japanese have installed converters enabling the Chinese plant to use the Fushun power. Much of the machinery in the Chinese plant, purchased from European and American companies, was unpaid for.

Kirin-Changchun and Kirin-Tunhwa Railways

These railways, both of which contain Japanese investments, were previously operated by the Chinese under separate boards of management. They have now been amalgamated under direct Japanese control, and all accounts and business transactions are handled directly by the Japanese manager.

Ssupingkai-Taonan and Taonan-Anganchi Railways

These two railways, also containing Japanese invested capital, were previously controlled and operated by the Chinese under separate managements. Both are now controlled and operated by the Japanese, and are understood to have been merged. It is also reported that the Chinese line connecting with the Taonan-Anganchi line and running northward to Kaoshun in Heilung-kiang province to the north of the Soviet-controlled Chinese Eastern Railway (constructed by the Provincial Government) has also been merged with the Ssupingkai-Taonan and Taonan-Anganchi lines under complete Japanese control.

Fengtien-Hailung and Hailung-Kirin Lines

Both Chinese constructed and controlled, but now subject to Japanese supervision. All through traffic over these lines from Kirin City through Mukden and thence to Tientsin and Peiping has been stopped owing to the Japanese cutting of the Sino-British Peiping-Mukden line in two places in the environs of Mukden. However, the Japanese have connected the P. M. (Peiping-Mukden Railway) line with the Japanese S. M. R. (South Manchuria Railway) line to enable the dispatch of armoured trains and troop trains over the Chinese lines.

Newchang Salt Gabelle Office

Forcibly taken over by the Japanese military following the Japanese occupation and large reserve funds on hand transferred to the account of the Mukden 'Peace Maintenance Committee' and used to finance this 'independent' organ under Japanese supervision.

Mukden Telephone Office

Before the Japanese occupation the Chinese municipality of Mukden operated its own telephone administration as distinct from the Japanese system in the Japanese concession. While it was possible to obtain a connection between the two services, the Chinese carefully guarded against an extension of the Japanese service into the Chinese-administered area. Since the Japanese occupation the Japanese authorities have established direct connection between the two services, and all telephone booths in the Japanese concession now have labels on the doors, 'Chinese' telephone and 'Japanese' telephone. In addition, the Japanese military maintain censors in the Chinese central office.

Before Japanese military occupation the Chinese had developed and were operating three extensive radio units. The long-wave station was completely wrecked on the night of the Japanese occupation, and shortly afterwards the main building was burned, although sup-

Mukden Radio Establishment

posedly guarded by the Japanese military. The other two stations were immediately closed down and have remained closed despite the protests of the foreign Consular body. The effect of the closure of the radio plants, plus the Japanese action in cutting all telegraph wires leading into China proper south of the Great Wall, has had the effect of forcing all external communication over the Japanese lines running from Mukden to Dairen and thence by cable to Japan, from where messages are relayed abroad by cable or Japanese radio.

The foregoing record indicates quite clearly that the Japanese have clinched their economic control of Manchuria, or, at least, those portions which are now controlled by the Japanese army, which includes all railways, excepting the Sino-British Peiping-Mukden line and the Soviet-controlled Chinese Eastern Line. Also it includes all provincial capitals where 'puppet' Chinese Administrations are functioning. Through their control of the Chinese financial organs, railways, and public utilities, as well as provincial capitals, the so-called 'open door' has been converted into a worthless scrap of paper. The large Euro-American companies which previously served the Chinese railways and public utilities are placed in an unenviable position from two standpoints: first, they are unable to collect outstanding accounts or settle claims against the previous Chinese Administration, which has been snuffed out, and, second, there is little prospect of future business in the face of complete or thinly camouflaged Japanese control. When the Japanese army, which completely dominates the Japanese financial and commercial establishment on the Asiatic continent, announces that it intends to maintain the 'open door' for world financial investment it means in practical effect that the Japanese, after they have consolidated their position, intend to enter the world's money markets for loans with which to develop their new holdings in Manchuria and Mongolia. Obviously there will be little opportunity for the foreign private firm to sell its goods unless it happens to handle a monopolised product that cannot be manufactured in Japan. A foreign consul long resident in Manchuria put it this way: 'The Japanese will maintain the "open door," but there will be so many Japanese standing in the door that nobody else will be able to enter'.

CHAPTER XIII

ATTEMPTS AT SETTLEMENT

China Appeals to the League

THE Chinese government appealed to the League of Nations Council on September 21, 1931, the Council then being in session, with both China and Japan sitting as members of the League and also of the Council, and invoked Article XI of the Covenant. The Council was asked to take immediate steps to prevent the further development of a situation which might endanger world peace; to re-establish the *status quo ante,* and to determine the amount and character of such reparations as might be found due to China for damages caused by Japanese military operations. China pledged that she would conform with whatever decisions the Council might make and accept whatever recommendations the Council under the Covenant might agree upon.

Japan at first opposed the invocation of Article XI, and insisted on direct negotiations. She also refused to accept the appointment of an international commission to look into the causes of the clash. After about ten days of deliberation and laborious efforts to get around Japanese objections, the Council adopted, on September 30, 1931, a resolution, in which Japan concurred, and the conditions of which Japan pledged herself to observe:

The Council—

1. Notes the replies of the Chinese and Japanese Governments

to the urgent appeal addressed to them by its President and the steps that have already been taken in response to that appeal;

2. Recognizes the importance of the Japanese Government's statement that it has no territorial designs in Manchuria;

3. Notes the Japanese representative's statement that his Government will continue, as rapidly as possible, the withdrawal of its troops, which has already been begun, into the railway zone in proportion as the safety of the lives and property of Japanese nationals is effectively assured and that it hopes to carry out this intention in full as speedily as may be;

4. Notes the Chinese representative's statement that his Government will assume responsibility for the safety of the lives and property of Japanese nationals outside that zone as the withdrawal of the Japanese troops continues and the Chinese local authorities and police forces are re-established;

5. Being convinced that both Governments are anxious to avoid taking any action which might disturb the peace and good understanding between the two nations, notes that the Chinese and Japanese representatives have given assurances that their respective Governments will take all necessary steps to prevent any extension of the scope of the incident or any aggravation of the situation;

6. Requests both parties to do all in their power to hasten the restoration of normal relations between them and for that purpose to continue and speedily complete the execution of the above-mentioned undertakings;

7. Requests both parties to furnish the Council at frequent intervals with full information as to the development of the situation.

8. Decides, in the absence of any unforeseen occurrence which might render an immediate meeting essential, to meet again at Geneva on Wednesday, October 14th, 1931, to consider the situation as it then stands;

9. Authorises its President to cancel the meeting of the Council fixed for October 14th should he decide, after consulting his colleagues, and more particularly the representatives of the two parties, that, in view of such information as he may have received from the parties or from other members of the Council as to the development of the situation, the meeting is no longer necessary.

What Japan Said and What Japan Did

On September 24 the Japanese delegate to the League
Council made the following declaration to the Council:

> The Japanese Government desires to state that it has withdrawn
> the greater part of its forces to the railway zone and that they are
> concentrated there. Outside that zone, only a few troops are, as a
> precautionary measure, quartered in the town of Mukden and at
> Kirin, and a small number of soldiers have been placed at certain
> points, these measures not constituting any military occupation.
>
> The Japanese forces are being withdrawn to the fullest extent
> which is at present allowed by the maintenance of the safety of Jap-
> anese nationals and the protection of the railways. The Japanese
> Government, which intends to withdraw its troops to the railway
> zone in proportion as the situation improves, feels confident that the
> Council, will, in this matter, trust the sincerity of its attitude.

On the same day, Japanese military planes bombed Chinchow, a Chinese city about 130 miles south of her railway
"zone," and two other cities, and Japanese troops advanced
to the northwest of Changchun. Three days later, on September 27, instead of withdrawing her troops as she had
promised, six train-loads of Japanese infantry arrived at
Kirin.

After the September 30 Resolution was adopted, and in
spite of it, Japan began to extend her military occupation.
Her military planes terrorized Chinese population over 150
miles beyond railway "zone" limits. Chinchow, the temporary headquarters of the Chinese administration, was
especially singled out for attack. Japanese planes repeatedly
dropped bombs which destroyed a section of the city
and killed a number of civilians. Meantime, Japanese
forces advanced further and further into Chinese territory,

and seized all Chinese government telegraph and telephone systems and railways. They aimed to destroy all Chinese organs of civil and military administration throughout the occupied territory.

Chang Hsueh-liang's One "Fault"

At the beginning of the occupation, General Honjo, Commander of Japanese forces in Manchuria, publicly announced that he intended to oust Chang Hsueh-liang who was the head of the Chinese Government of Manchuria and an official of the National Government of China. When Mukden, the capital of Manchuria was taken, Chang made Chinchow his temporary headquarters. Japanese military planes dropped handbills, as well as bombs, to intimidate the Chinese people. The text of the handbills distributed over Chinchow was as follows:

Chang Hsueh-liang, that most rapacious wanton, stinking youth, is still failing to realize his odiousness and has established a Provisional Mukden Government at Chinchow to plot intrigues in the territories which are safely under the rule of the troops of the Great Japanese Empire, when the heart of the Manchurian masses is no longer with him, his ground is lost, and the four provinces of the Northeast are going to revolt against him. The Imperial Army, which, in accordance with the principles of justice, is endeavoring to safeguard its interests and to protect the masses, will never recognize the Provisional Government of Chang Hsueh-liang at Chinchow, and therefore, it is obliged to take drastic measures to suppress such a government. The people of Chinchow should submit to the kindness and power of the army of the Great Japanese Empire and should oppose and prevent the establishment of Chang Hsueh-liang's government, otherwise they will be considered as decidedly opposing the army of the Great Japanese Empire, in which case the army will ruthlessly destroy Chinchow. The people of Chinchow are hereby enjoined carefully to consider their situation and to take such decisions as they will deem wise.

The New York *Times* reported on October 22, 1931:

Marshal Chang Hsueh-liang today was advised by Japanese military authorities that 437 cases containing his household furniture and personal effects had been dispatched from Mukden to Tientsin. An earlier communication on the same subject made it clear that Marshal Chang's presence in Manchuria was not desired and, in the Japanese view, there was no excuse for his returning.

Thus Japan arrogated to herself the right of deciding who should and who should not be an official in Chinese territory. Chang Hsueh-liang's one "fault" was that, in 1928, he did not heed the warning of the Japanese envoy who advised him not to join the central government of China.

"Unanimous Minus One Vote"

The League Council found it necessary to convene again on October 13th. The United States Government which had given its approval of the September 30th Resolution signified its willingness to appoint a representative to sit with the Council, if invited. Japan strenuously objected to the invitation. Finally, by a 13 to 1 vote, the United States was invited to participate. The Council then invoked the Pact of Paris (Briand-Kellogg Pact) on October 17th.

Japan now attached two entirely new conditions to the withdrawal of her troops: (1), China to give effect to all existing railway treaties; and (2), China to agree to settle certain fundamental principles. The Council requested

Japan on October 24th to define the fundamental principles she referred to in her counter-resolution. This Japan refused to do. Japan's counter-resolution was defeated by a 13 to 1 vote. On the same day the Council passed its own resolution "unanimously minus one vote," that of Japan. In this resolution the Council reaffirmed its earlier resolution and called upon Japan immediately to begin troop withdrawal and to complete withdrawal by November 16th.

The New York *Times* correspondent commented on the meeting as follows:

"Japan is Isolated"

Never was a national in an international dispute made to feel her isolation and the force of combined disapproval as Japan was in the closing debates of this Council meeting. And seldom has any nation so obstinately resisted all along, every wile, threat, persuasion, and cajolement, as did Japan through Kenkichi Yoshizawa, her delegate, who kept repeating that he could not accept because his government did not agree with the delegate from Spain, from France, from Britain, nor with any of the others . . .

In many respects, as a number of the Council members emphasized in their speeches today, this Far Eastern problem has become the pivotal point of the world political situation at this moment, because its effective solution has become essential to the approach of nearly all the great problems which the Occidental nations are now facing.

Its bearing upon the disarmament problem was repeatedly considered in the debates, and it also involves the whole efficacy of the international machinery for preventing war, of questions of security, boundaries and the sanctity of international treaties themselves. Lord Reading even went so far as to say, before he left Geneva, that the Manchurian problem must be solved before the world can hope to deal successfully with the economic crisis . . .

'I see great danger,' said Senor de Madariaga, 'in a national claiming the right to stay in territory, in which one is not entitled to be on the plea of insecurity.' And afterward, referring to the preamble of the League Covenant, which provides for open and honorable relations between nations, he added: 'So far as open relations are concerned I have to admit that I am greatly disappointed by the attitude of the Japanese government.'

Even Mr. Briand was moved to the unkind reflection that 'public opinion would find it difficult to admit that military occupation could be assigned to the category of pacific means' in settling disputes." (New York *Times,* October 25, 1931).

"Japanese Army Ran Amuck"

Whether the Japanese army got entirely out of control of the civilian branch of the government, or whether Japan created this impression to evade responsibility, is unimportant here. The fact is that the Japanese army had thrown to the winds all treaty obligations and the solemn pledges of the Japanese Government and had gone on with feverish speed and ruthlessness to extend its occupation in Manchuria and to provoke clashes in other parts of China. On November 9th Tientsin was shelled. Armed gunmen used the Japanese concession in that city to harass Chinese police. When the latter attempted to disarm the gunmen, Japanese troops opened fire and shelled the Chinese section of the city. On November 13th Japanese forces took Tsitsihar, the capital of Heilungkiang, a city over 370 miles north of the Japanese railway zone.

When the League re-convened in Paris on November 16th it found that Japan had not only violated her pledges, but had created a far more serious situation. Even while the Council was meeting, Japanese forces were advancing

towards Chinchow. The Council proposed to neutralize
the Chinchow area on November 25th, 1931. China welcomed the proposal at once. Japan rejected it. On Novem-
tion "unanimously minus one vote," that of Japan. In this

> On the strength of apparently authentic reports that Japanese
> troops were advancing on the Manchurian provisional capital at Chin-
> chow, the State Department was preparing tonight to put Japanese
> good faith to the test of world opinion.
> Within forty-eight hours of announcements indicating highly
> promising peace prospects in Manchuria, Henry L. Stimson, Secretary
> of State, served notice in effect that an attack on Chinchow would be
> in direct violation of a pledge given Tuesday to the United States
> Government by Baron Kijuro Shidehara, Japanese Foreign Minister,
> speaking for himself, the Japanese Minister of War and the Japa-
> nese chief of staff . . .

The report that Mr. Stimson said that "the Japanese
Army had run amuck" aroused a storm of resentment in
Japan. The Japanese press and Foreign Office did not think
that the American Secretary of State had any right to doubt
the good faith of the Japanese Government. But in less
than five weeks Japan took Chinchow.

"Neutral Powers Do Not Understand"

Since the League Council more than once voted over
the objections of Japan, Japanese officials repeatedly complained that the neutral powers did not understand the
Manchurian situation. General Jiro Tamon of Tsitsihar
fame frankly informed the United Press correspondent on
November 21st that "The actions of the League are very
annoying. They know nothing of Manchurian affairs." It

was a fact that the information which the League got from neutral observers often contradicted that given by Japan. Before attacking Chinchow, Japan circulated rumors to the effect that there was a Chinese troop concentration there for an offensive. The New York *Herald Tribune* correspondent reported to the contrary on December 5, 1931:

> Japanese reports that Chinese troops from Chinchow have been advancing northeastward along the Peiping-Mukden Railway toward Mukden are false, this correspondent was informed by the neutral military observers on the spot when he arrived here this evening.
>
> Contrary to recent Japanese military reports, no Chinese reinforcements have been sent forth of the Great Wall, the boundary between China proper and the Manchurian provinces, nor have the Chinese troops stationed in the Chinchow area, the last territory remaining under Chinese control in southern Manchuria, been advanced toward Mukden.
>
> Throughout this correspondent's eight-hour journey today from Mukden to Chinchow, aboard the first Tientsin-bound train to leave Mukden for a week, he saw little evidence of any Chinese preparation for a military offensive.
>
> The neutral observers here, who have been investigating the military situation thoroughly since November 24th, are Lieutenant Colonel Nelson E. Margetts, military attache of the American Legation at Peiping; First Lieutenant Harry S. Aldrich, American student interpreter attached to the military attache's office; the British Military Attache from Peiping and two assistants; the French consul, the French air service attache, and one interpreter, and the German Secretary of Legation from Peiping . . .

Boycott Is the Direct Result

The Chinese economic boycott is the direct result of Japan's military occupation of Manchuria. It is a natural expression of indignation. The term itself may appear formidable. In reality it is practiced by individuals every day. For instance, when an employee of Jones' Store treats Mr. A. discourteously, Mr. A. decides not to trade there any more. That is a boycott.

The recent boycott movement began in July 1931, as a result of the anti-Chinese riots. It gathered strength and spread all over the country after Japan occupied Manchuria. Replying to the Japanese Memorandum of October 9th on boycott, the Chinese Government stated,

> Freedom to choose one's purchases is an individual right with which no government can interfere, and while it is the duty of every government to protect foreign nationals, it is bound neither by any recognized standard of governance, nor by any principle of international law, to prohibit or punish the exercise of an elementary right of citizenship. If there be any responsibility at all in the matter, it entirely lies with Japan since the Wanpaoshan incident, which created this general prejudice against Japanese merchandise.

No government, however strong, can compel its people to buy from their enemies. Furthermore, for the sake of its own existence, it must not show that it is entirely unsympathetic toward a nation-wide spontaneous movement of the people. A boycott does harm to both the boycotter and the boycotted. The only way to stop the boycott is to remove the cause,—the military occupation of Chinese territory.

In December, 1931, Japanese exports to China were 80 per cent less than in December, 1930.

Navy Vied for Glory

Several interpretations have been advanced for the widespread Japanese naval operations outside of Manchuria. One is that the Japanese Army had scored such a complete mili-

tary success in Manchuria that the Navy would want also
to prove its mettle. Another theory is that if Japan could
take Shanghai and Nanking, China would yield to any
terms. A third theory points out that Japan would gain
what she desires if she could force China to declare war. If
she could take Shanghai, according to a fourth theory, Japan
would be in a position, not only to break the boycott, but
also to bargain on Manchuria. Whatever the reason, Japan
planned in October to control China's seacoast and the
Yangtze River.

As early as October, 1931, there were premonitions of
Japanese naval action.

Two Japanese destroyers arrived here today and two others were
on their way to reinforce Japan's flotilla on the Yangtze River in the
face of Japanese officials' fears that serious trouble would break out
against their nationals in many ports.

The Japanese exodus from various Chinese cities developing since
trouble started openly two weeks ago with the occupation of southern
Manchuria by Japanese troops quickened a little today. (New York
Sun, October 5, 1931.)

Feverish anxiety reigns tonight in all Chinese official circles because of the fear that Japan may land marines at Shanghai and take
over the policing of Nantao, Chapei, and other portions of the native
city.

Chinese banks, bond houses and brokerage houses did virtually
no business today, dealing being paralyzed by rumors which distorted
the annual rendezvous of the Japanese Navy at Sasebo for its regular
manoeuvres into wild reports that the Japanese were mobilized for
an attack on all Chinese seaports. This report even reached Nanking, where the fortifications were strengthened and Chinese gun-
boats took up positions in the Yangtze River.

The anxiety was intensified by dispatches from Tokyo officially
declaring that Japan was forwarding a sharp protest to Nanking
over the growth of the anti-Japanese movement all over China, the

virtual severance of economic relations and Nanking's alleged un-
willingness or inability to curb the agitation, constituting a danger to
Japanese lives and properties in China. Late tonight dispatches from
Sasebo declared that the Japanese Navy Office had been ordered to
prepare for mobilization and to have warships ready to reach the
coast of China within twenty-four hours if necessary.   (Hallett
Abend, special cable to the New York *Times,* October 7, 1931.)

"Insult" to Japan

So far there had been no retaliation upon Japanese subjects, except for one incident in Hongkong, in spite of
Japan's military operations in Manchuria. The Chinese
people had exercised unusual self-control, but the Japanese
residents did not make it easy for the Chinese to do so. The
following is a typical example of how the Japanese behaved
in China during the crisis:

Tsingtao, China, Jan. 13 (AP)—Five hundred steel-helmeted
marines, carrying fixed bayonets, patrolled the streets of Tsingtao
today while thousands of Chinese fled the city in fear of a possible
recurrence of yesterday's rioting.

The trouble started when the Chinese newspaper, Kuo-Min-Jih
Pao, said the recent attempt by a Korean on the life of Emperor
Hirohito indicated Korea's desire for independence.

Japanese residents interpreted this as an insult to the Emperor
and stormed the newspaper plant. Firing revolvers, they thronged
into the building and the Chinese staff fled. Attempts were made
to burn the place, but they were unsuccessful.

Later several thousand Japanese paraded behind their nation's
flag, demanding further action against the newspaper. After the
parade the demonstrators made another attack, this time burning the
newspaper building and the headquarters of the Kuomintang (Chinese Nationalist Party) as well.

The Japanese Consul announced that he was unable to control his
national and that with the permission of the Chinese Mayor he has

asked for the marines. They turned the Japanese consulate into a fortress, bristling with machine guns mounted on its flat roof. (New York *Times,* January 14, 1932.)

Super Salesmanship in the Far East!

—From *The Cleveland Plain Dealer.*

CHAPTER XIV

SHANGHAI

THERE had occurred a number of street brawls between Chinese and Japanese in Shanghai. In one of them, one Japanese monk was seriously wounded and later died. This led to the Japanese attack on January 28, 1932.

Shiozawa to "Preserve Peace"

On January 27 Consul-General Murai had presented an ultimatum to Mayor Wu Teh-chen requiring complete acceptance of the Japanese demands—a step which was reinforced by the threat of punitive action made independently by the Japanese Admiral Shiozawa. Later on the same day, Mayor Wu Teh-chen closed the headquarters of the anti-Japanese boycott association; and on January 28th, four hours before the ultimatum's expiration limit of 6 P.M. (Shanghai time), he unconditionally accepted the Japanese demands. Consul-General Murai thereupon stated that the Chinese assurances were satisfactory. Several hours later, however, Admiral Shiozawa issued a declaration, apparently on his own responsibility, announcing his decision to 'take necessary military action to preserve peace and order in the Chapei district.' Shortly after midnight Japanese marines issued from the International Settlement and invaded Chapei, thus disregarding previous official Japanese assurances that no military steps would be taken without twenty-four hours' notice to the Shanghai consular authorities.

Meeting with unexpected stiff resistance from the veteran Cantonese force commanded by General Tsai Ting-chai, the Japanese marines made slight progress in the night hours. Bombs dropped into Chapei by Japanese airplanes throughout January 29th set large areas on fire. The Chinese civilians in Chapei (normally 200,000) were forced to choose between the bullet-swept streets and the spreading fire; the total number of deaths will never be accurately known. In the course of the action, Japanese bombs demolished the Com-

mercial Press—China's mammoth publishing house which has printed
the majority of Chinese publications, including the Nationalist text-
books denounced by Japan. Fighting continued for thirty-six hours
until noon of January 30—when the Japanese commander admitted
failure by halting his offensive, and a period of desultory sniping set
in. The interim was utilized by the Shanghai consular authorities
to effect a truce, but all attempts to achieve this end have thus far
failed.

Aside from the actual losses to foreign life and property, which
are not yet full estimated, the gravest international issue is raised by
Japan's use of the Settlement as a base of military operations. This
issue was rendered more acute on January 31st when the Japanese
proceeded to disarm the Settlement police within the Hongkew area.
Immediate protests against this action were addressed to Tokyo by
Great Britain and the United States. Despite official assurances from
Tokyo denying the intention to use the Settlement as a military base,
fortifications, manned exclusively by the Japanese, were erected
around the Hongkew area on February 2nd.

On February 2 the United States and England submitted a com-
prehensive peace proposal to Japan and China. The first principal
points of this proposal are as follows: cessation of all acts of violence;
no further mobilization or preparation for hostilities; withdrawal of
both Japanese and Chinese combatants from all points of mutual contact in Shanghai; protection of the Settlement by establishment of a
neutral zone to be policed by neutrals under consular authority; and
prompt advances toward negotiations to settle outstanding Sino-
Japanese controversies, with the aid of neutral observers or partici-
pants, in the spirit of the Pact of Paris and the League resolutions of
December 9. On the same day, at an extraordinary session of the
League Council in Geneva, M. Tardieu and Signor Grandi seconded
the Anglo-American move on behalf of France and Italy. (T. A.
Bisson, in Foreign Policy Bulletin, February 5, 1932.)

An "Undeclared" War

Japan massed over 40 warships, 60,000 men, and over
200 military planes to capture Shanghai. China immediately
requested the League Council to act and invoked Articles

X and XV of the Covenant. Under Article XV, the Council at once authorized its Secretary-General to make necessary arrangements for a full investigation. A Committee of Inquiry was appointed to act on the spot. It was composed of the official representatives of League members, who were instructed to report on the circumstances and nature of the Japanese attack. The following is the Second Report of the Committee at Shanghai:

Since 3rd February a state of open war exists, any pretence of a truce being abandoned. Firing continues intermittently, both in the Chapei and Woosung area, with the use of artillery and, on the side of the Japanese, by aerial bombardment. The offensive is entirely in the hands of the Japanese whose declared object is to capture the Woosung forts and drive all the Chinese troops a considerable distance from Shanghai.

Commenting on the situation in Shanghai, the British delegate, at the meeting of the Council on February 2, said.

His Majesty's Government in the United Kingdom feels it is impossible that the present situation in the Far East should be allowed to continue. Every day brings news of some fresh incident of the utmost gravity. Fighting over a wide area is practically continuous. Shanghai is the scene of a series of conflicts in which rifles and machine guns, artillery and aeroplanes are taking part. War in everything but name is in progress.

The proposal for peace by the British, American, French, Italian and German Governments was accepted by China *in toto,* but was rejected by Japan in all its essential features.

Appeal by Twelve Powers

Japan continued to use the International Settlement as her base of operation against the Chinese in spite of protests by neutral powers. As the situation went from bad to worse, the twelve members of the Council, other than the parties to the dispute, made the following appeal to the Japanese Government on February 17, 1932:

> To make a pressing appeal to the Government of Japan to recognize the very special responsibilities for forbearance and restraint which devolves upon it in the present conflict, in virtue of the position of Japan as a Member of the League of Nations and a Permanent Member of the Council . . . Japan has an incalculable responsibility before the public opinion of the world to be just and restrained in her relations with China. She has already acknowledged this responsibility in most solemn terms by becoming one of the signatories to the Nine Power Treaty of 1922 whereby the contracting Powers expressly agreed to respect the sovereignty, the independence and the territorial and administrative integrity of China. The Twelve Members of the Council appeal to Japan's high sense of honour to recognize the obligations of her special position and of the confidence which the nations have placed in her as a partner in the organization and maintenance of peace.

This earnest appeal was answered by Japan with an ultimatum at 9 P.M. the next day (February 18) demanding the complete evacuation of Chinese troops from their first lines by 7 A.M., February 20, and complete evacuation by 5 P.M. on the same day to a distance of 12.5 miles (20 kilometres) beyond the boundaries of the International Settlement; the permanent dismantling of the Woosung forts and all the other fortifications and military works in the evacuated areas; failing which the Japanese commander would take necessary action.

The Council met to consider the Japanese ultimatum on the eve of the battle (February 19). The President, M. Paul-Boncour, made a stirring last minute appeal to the Japanese government:

You (the Japanese Representative) have told us that as soon as the Japanese have, by the operations now impending, ensured the security of their nationals, there will be no question of their remaining on the ground won by their troops. That being so, I ask, and with a sincerity and emotion which you will certainly find in my words, whether there is not an appalling inconsistency between your freedom from territorial interests and the fact that a battle is about to be joined and that the field will be strewn with dead, whereas, whatever the outcome, it follows from your quite unambiguous statement, that the Japanese will evacuate the field as soon as they have achieved their object.

You pointed out, briefly, but perfectly clearly, the method by which hostilities could be prevented. You said that as soon as the fighting was over, neutral forces could easily guarantee order in the neutral zone between the two parties, thus assuring the safety of both.

In these circumstances I wonder whether, in order to avert the impending struggle, it would not be possible to agree at once upon a solution which would be put into effect later.

If you could prevent the ultimatum from expiring within a few hours, what an example you would have given, what a service you would have rendered to the League! In the simplest possible words, I beg you to do so with a conviction which you certainly cannot fail to recognize.

This appeal also fell on deaf ears. In the words of the Third Report of the Shanghai Committee:

During the night, February 19–February 20, Japanese reinforcements were moved from their base in the International Settlement to the Japanese lines, and after preliminary reconnaissance which satisfied the Japanese that the Chinese had not evacuated their lines in conformity with the demand, the Japanese opened attack February 20 at 7.30 A.M. in the Kiangwan and Woosung areas. Hostilities continued the whole day.

Acts of "Self-Defense"

Whatever may be Japan's official explanation or pretext, the following was what she did as reported from an unimpeachable source:

REFUGEE CAMP BOMBED, 50 DIE, SOME OF FRIGHT

10,000 Flood Sufferers Scattered by Repeated Raids by
Japanese Flyers

SHANGHAI, Feb. 11—The most startling chapter in the history of the Japanese bombing operations here yet brought to light was disclosed today by Sir John Hope Simpson, Director General of the Chinese National Flood Relief Committee (designated by the League), in a letter of today's date sent to T. V. Soong, Chairman of Flood Relief and Chinese Minister of Finance.

The letter details repeated Japanese air bombing of a Chinese flood relief camp which, over a period of several days, resulted in the deaths of fifty refugees. The letter follows:

I have to report to you that the camp for flood refugees situated on Yuiying Road, two miles northwest of the North Station on the border of Chapei, contained on January 26th, 10,399 refugees and 49 members of the floor relief staff.

During the first Japanese air bombardment, on January 29, 2,000 refugees fled, 8,000 remaining for food and shelter.

On February 5, at noon, the Japanese bombed the camp, killing one woman and one boy and wounding four. Some of our hospital patients died of fright. Most of the refugees fled, a few hundred remaining, the majority of whom were sick and aged.

On the following day, the bombing was repeated, killing 48 refugees, mostly hospital patients, excepting 20 persons. The survivors were removed, but the camp was again bombed on February 7 and 8, even after all had withdrawn.

I have lodged a protest with the Japanese Consulate-General against this bombing, which was unnecessary, inhuman and of no military advantage. The continuous bombing of homeless refugees has resulted only in the sacrifice of fifty innocent lives."
(New York *Herald Tribune,* February 12, 1932.)

Since the 3rd of February, a state of open war has existed, any pretense of a truce being abandoned. The offensive is entirely in the hands of the Japanese, whose declared object is to capture the Woosung forts and drive all Chinese troops a considerable distance from Shanghai . . . The Japanese naval authorities took complete control of the Hongkew district inside the Settlement, barricaded streets, disarmed the police, and paralyzed all other municipal activities of the Settlement authorities, including the fire brigade . . . Numerous excesses, including summary executions, were committed by the (Japanese) marines and reservists . . . A reign of terror resulted and almost the entire non-Japanese population of the area ran away.

Owing to the large number of Chinese who were believed to have been arrested or put to death by the Japanese, and of whom no trace could be found, the Municipal Council on the 5th of February asked the consular body to approach the Japanese authorities with the view to an inquiry. The Japanese Consul admitted excesses had been committed by his nationals at the time when feeling was running high . . . and he agreed that persons arrested as suspects by naval authorities within the Settlement should be handed over to the municipal police. This was accordingly done, but the number of Chinese still unaccounted for is very large. The municipal police already have collected details of about 100 cases. (Foreign Policy Association Bulletin, Feb. 19, 1932.)

The "Independent" Government

While the attention of the world was concentrating on Shanghai, Japan was consolidating her position in Manchuria. On March 9, 1932, Japanese army officers put Henry Pu Yi on the throne of Manchoukuo. Henry Pu Yi, the deposed Emperor of the Manchu régime, had been living in the Japanese concession in Tientsin for over ten years. He had recently been conveyed from Tientsin to Dairen on a Japanese destroyer, escorted by Colonel Daihara of the Japanese army. Under this "dictator" there are a number of officials who are like Yuan Chin-Kai:

Yuan Chin-Kai installed with ceremony by the Japanese as head of an independent provincial government in Mukden on Tuesday, charged in a secret interview today that he was forced to do the bidding of the Japanese, and that his government, nominally Manchurian, was in effect nothing but a Japanese Government.

Yuan, ostensibly an ally of Japan and false to the Government of Chang Hsueh-liang, nominal Governor of Manchuria, asserted that he was doing his best to further the interests of Manchuria following the ousting of the regular government.

Interviewed in his dingy offices, Yuan spoke in whispers to avoid being overheard by the Japanese. He closed the door cautiously after a careful reconnaissance to see if Japanese agents were in the building.

'The Japanese,' Yuan said, 'controlled his government and dictated its policies.

'They would have imprisoned me and installed persons who would have no regard for Manchuria's welfare if I had refused,' he said, explaining why he had accepted the post. 'I am trying to do my best for the Chinese and avert more serious trouble. I know the Japanese are trying their hardest to restore a Manchu emperor, but I have nothing to do with it. When I assumed office I had no idea things would go so far. The Japanese immediately pressed me to negotiate a Manchurian settlement, but I refused and still refuse. I would like Chang Hsueh-liang's return, but that is now impossible.

'The Japanese compelled me to do many things contrary to my wishes, including the ceremony of installation and the proclamation severing relations with the regular Manchurian government, but others might have done worse.'

When the correspondent left, his car was trailed by a Japanese detective, who had followed it to Yuan's office before the interview. (Victor Keen, New York *Herald Tribune*, November 15, 1931.)

Japan now confronts the world with an alleged *fait accompli* in Manchuria. This illegal, but *de facto*, government may claim the right to transfer rights and conclude treaties with Japan, if not eventually to incorporate itself as part of the Japanese Empire.

PART THREE

THE SIGNIFICANCE

The Baby's Born
Westerman in Ohio State Journal

CHAPTER XV

JAPAN'S *FAIT ACCOMPLI*

THE destruction of Chapei, a thickly populated section of Shanghai, on January 29, 1932, was the turning point in the Sino-Japanese conflict. Japan had committed similar acts at Mukden and Chinchow. But Manchuria seems to be so remote. There are very few Americans and Europeans there and the investments of American and European powers excepting Russia are not large. With Shanghai it is different. Here is an international port and one of the most important shipping centers. About sixty per cent of China's foreign trade go through Shanghai. A war threatens not only the trade of all nations but also the very life and property of a large number of American and European residents. And war at its worst was brought to the front door of the International Settlement. They ceased to be news-readers and became eye-witnesses.

Through this group of official and unofficial representatives of practically every civilized country the rest of the world has been able to get a more vivid and truthful picture of the situation. They began to know the Japanese, not through Japan's official statements nor censored dispatches, but by the actions of the Japanese forces and civilians on the spot.

The smoke of cannons has lifted over Chapei. This once thickly populated and thriving section of Shanghai is now in charred ruins. The work of war correspondents appears to be finished, but the task of statesmen and historians has just begun. They must take stock of what is left of international law and peace treaties. "War" and "self-defense" must be redefined. The world cannot stand, nor does it want another world war; but how could such a conflict be prevented, and the causes of war be removed? We must, then, pause and analyze the far-reaching causes and effects and the fundamental issues involved in the present crisis in China.

In attempting to grasp the significance of the conflict between China and Japan it will be found that Manchuria holds the key to the understanding of the true character and significance of the conflict between China and Japan.

W. W. Willoughby's comments on Japan's policy and methods of 1915 largely hold good as to what her actions during the present crisis signify:

In 1915 came the Twenty-One Demands by Japan upon China, by the presentation of which Japan made it no longer possible for her to deny without insulting the intelligence of those to whom the denial might be addressed, that it was her desire to dominate China politically as well as economically.

The political and military weakness of China, and, after the Russian Revolution of 1917, of Eastern Siberia as well, has furnished the opportunity; the natural resources and agricultural products of China and Russia have furnished the temptation; and her own increasing population and lack of mineral resources have furnished Japan with the incentive for her aggressive imperialistic policies.

Upon the other hand there was Japan, with a strong, centralized, bureaucratic, monarchical government, largely under the control of

militarists, with undisguised imperialistic policies eager to widen
Japan's political and economic influence and control if not Japan's
sovereignty, and exhibiting little regard for the legal or ethical rights
of other peoples whose interests might stand in the way of the realization of its own ambitions.

During the crisis there have been two wars going on
side by side, military and diplomatic. While diplomats were
exchanging notes and wrangling over technicalities Japanese
forces were losing no time in accomplishing their objectives.
They went about their task so ruthlessly and efficiently that
even the Japanese Foreign Office and the Japanese Delegate
to the League of Nations have had considerable difficulty in
following the Japanese military operations for which they
have been called upon to offer post-mortem pretexts and
explanations. The war clique of Japan knew from the beginning that the rest of the world was not in a position to
intervene by force. In the past, after boundaries had been
changed, and small and weak countries annexed and parti-
tioned by conquest, the world usually accepted the *fait
accompli*. It was on this assumption that the Japanese army
proceeded with a well planned campaign in Manchuria.

Two-Thirds of Manchuria Conquered

When the Japanese forces started out on September 18,
1931, Japan controlled only about one-half of one per cent of
Manchurian territory, i.e., about 1,400 square miles. Since
then they have occupied over 200,000 square miles, over two-
thirds of Manchuria. This region contains the richest coal,
iron and oil deposits and also holds the key positions through

which the resources of the country find their outlet to China proper and other countries.

The conservative estimate by neutral observers is that there are at least 65,000 troops in the occupied territory. They are divided into small detachments stationed at all strategic points. Wireless stations and airplane units keep the detachments in touch about uprisings which are being put down with the utmost brutality in order to strike terror to the hearts of the Chinese people. Although, technically, there is no war and no martial law is declared, the whole area is ruled according to the laws and regulations of the Japanese army which has assigned to itself the right to suppress "bandits" and decide who are "bandits" and how they shall be punished.

Even if the territory were restored to China today the pre-war conditions could not be re-established for years. In the first place many public institutions have been completely destroyed, such as Northeastern and Feng Yung Universities. The Japanese have taken over all important government and private industries and businesses. (See Chapter XII.) Secondly, pursuing the same tactics she employed during the years after the Russo-Japanese War, she has been extending her "Zone" and confiscating private land for "military necessity" and on other grounds.

In the regions in Manchuria under Japanese occupation a move has been started by Japanese land corporations falsely and forcibly to establish titles to land, now legally held by Chinese. The Showa Agricultural Corporation, a Japanese concern, has written letters to eleven villages, including Huang-Ka-Tun, Niu-Hsin-Tun and others, claiming that the land belonged to two Japanese who had transferred it to the Corporation several years ago, and ordered the tenants to apply for certificates issued by the Corporation, threatening eviction if this is not complied with. On November 11th, the said Corporation erected boundary signs with the following words: 'This Land Property of the Showa Corporation.'   (Letter, dated November 28th, 1931, from the Chinese Delegation to the Secretary-General of the League of Nations.)

Japan Controls over Half of the Railways

Before September 18th, Japan controlled about 689 miles of railways; now she controls 2,314 miles, over half of the total number of railways in Manchuria. All Chinese railways are now in her hands. The only railway not directly under Japanese control is the Chinese Eastern Railway in Northern Manchuria.

Through her absolute control of the transportation system she is in a position to dictate prices on agricultural products and also to discriminate in favor of her own trade as she has always done on the South Manchuria Railway and through the ports under her control.

Her Strategic Position

Manchuria is the helmet of China. From Mukden a foreign power can at any time threaten Peiping and Tientsin, and, from Dairen, the province of Shantung, China's head and throat. For centuries, and especially since the Sung Dynasty, alien races have successfully used Manchuria as their base of military operations against China.

With all the railways in South Manchuria under her control, Japan has succeeded in carrying out her long cherished

plan of consolidating her strategic position. She is already
linking Korea and Manchuria. Her next step will be to
extend the Taonan line to Jehol. In this way she will be
able to rush large forces to China within 48 hours from
Korea and through Dairen to points on the Great Wall and
the Siberian border. In her present position Japan could use
military pressure more effectively to impose her will upon
China in direct negotiations.

Economic Dominance

As a result of her stupendous action of "self-defense" she
has gained a territory that is one and a half times the area
of Japan proper. The agricultural output, forests and min-
erals in this territory will more than meet her own requirements for food supply and raw materials. The land and
mines that she has confiscated are being operated without
capital investment and not much overhead. Public utilities
and banking have already for some time been in Japanese
hands. Thus, she has created for herself ideal conditions to
monopolize trade and exploit the resources in Manchuria.

Colonization

On the one hand, the "Independent" government has
already adopted measures to discourage Chinese immigrants
from coming to Manchuria, while, on the other hand, a
system of land registration is being carried out under
Japanese supervision. Those Chinese who were killed during the hostilities and those who fled away, will not be able
to claim their property according to the regulations. Of

course, the Japanese supervisors and advisers will pass on the validity of Chinese claims. This is precisely the way how the Japanese confiscated desirable land and other property of the Koreans after the annexation of Korea.

Cables from Tokyo and Manchuria to the New York *Times* (March 21, 1932) indicate that "there is a well-financed movement in Japanese officialdom to assist in financing Japanese settlers in Manchuria."

Political Fictions

On March 9th, the Japanese Foreign Ministry, speaking before the Japanese Diet, made a laborious explanation that the independent state was an autonomous movement. The next day the Japanese Minister of War told the Diet that a larger Japanese force should be stationed in Manchuria to make sure of the "desirable consummation" of the Manchuria problem.

Due to Japanese censorship and military pressure, the voice of the Chinese people in Manchuria has been muzzled. But thousands of Chinese who were driven out by the Japanese invasion have expressed their conviction. The following are two of their messages transmitted to the League of Nations Assembly:

March 10, 1932.

We, the provincials of the Three Eastern Provinces of China (Manchuria), solemnly declare that the independence movement in the Japanese occupied territory is purely under the Japanese manipulation. For months past the world has been aware of the frantic efforts being made by the Japanese to work up a semblance of popular enthusiasm, but the only response has come from their hirelings and people under coercion. The leaders are not free agents. We appeal to the world to discountenance such a manipulated movement engineered entirely by the Japanese as a step forward to realize their territorial ambitions.

Signed: Chairman of the Committee of the Provincials of the Three Eastern Provinces of China:

CHIN EN-CHI,
LU KUANG-CHI
WANG HUA-YI.

(League of Nations Document A (Extr.) 40.1932.VII)

March 11, 1932.

We, the Members of the Faculty and the Students' Union of the Northeastern University, Mukden, compelled to abandon the university plant under Japanese military pressure and carrying on in temporary quarters at Peiping, strongly denounce the new independent state, set up in the Northeastern Provinces of China under Japanese manipulation in utter disregard of the wishes of the Chinese people. Such action constitutes a violent attack on China's territorial integrity and makes a mockery of the principle of self-determination. We earnestly solicit the support of the Governments and peoples of the world in our determined effort to defeat Japan's aggressions.

Signed: For the Faculty:
NING EN-CHENG, *Chief Secretary.*

For the Students' Union:
LIU TE-LIN, *Chairman.*

(League of Nations Document A (Extr.) 47.1932.VIII)

Attitude of the Powers

The United States Government declared on January 7, 1932,

That it cannot admit the legality of any situation *de facto,* nor does it intend to recognize any treaty or agreement entered into between those governments, or grants thereof, which may impair the treaty rights of the United States or its citizens in China, including those which relate to the sovereignty, the independence or the territorial and administrative integrity of the Republic of China, or to the international policy relative to China, commonly known as the Open Door policy;

And that it does not intend to recognize any situation, treaty or agreement which may be brought about by means contrary to the covenants and obligations of the Pact of Paris of Aug. 27, 1928, to which treaty both China and Japan, as well as the United States, are parties.

The League of Nations Assembly adopted on March 11, 1932, a resolution which declares in Article I,

The Assembly proclaims the binding nature of the principles and provisions referred to above and declares that it is incumbent upon the Members of the League of Nations not to recognize any situation, treaty or agreement which may be brought about by means contrary to the Covenant of the League of Nations or to the Pact of Paris.

What effect these two declarations will eventually have upon the Manchurian situation, time will tell. So far it has exerted no appreciable influence upon Japan.

But there is a force that is stronger than international law, nay, even stronger than armies and navies. This is the inherent desire of the people for liberty and independence. How long can Japan hold in subjugation 30 million Chinese people who, though temporarily inarticulate and helpless, are of the same blood and culture with over 400,000,000 of their kinsmen, and who, with the rest of their fellow-countrymen, are determined to struggle to the end for their national integrity.

Already "bandit" uprisings in Manchuria are multiplying day after day. Unless Manchuria is restored to China without delay the trouble is but beginning. Nor will Japan find it as profitable as she anticipated, for economic development is not possible in a land with a hostile population. She should have learned this lesson from the annexation of Korea. But in Manchuria Japan has the rest of China to contend with. History has yet to produce an example in which a foreign power has ruled successfully by force a large population that has developed a consciousness of nationality.

But Can You Control Him?

CHAPTER XVI

JAPAN'S NINETEENTH CENTURY IDEAS AND METHODS

ONE significant revelation from the crisis is that the ideas and methods of Japanese diplomacy belong to the last century. Other nations have advanced; new attitudes have been developed taking the place of the Nineteenth Century ideas and methods which have been outgrown and discarded. That is the chief reason why Japan has found herself diplomatically isolated. The following are some of the examples which illustrate the attitude and tactics of the Japanese government:

Geographical Propinquity

In spite of her solemn pledge to respect the independence of Korea, Japan annexed that country in 1910 on the pretext of geographical propinquity, Korea being near to Japan, and therefore, Japan said she must control it on account of special interests arising from the special positions of the two countries. Since then Japan has claimed the right of controlling Manchuria and Inner Mongolia for the same reason because Inner Mongolia is next to Manchuria, Manchuria is next to Korea, and Korea is near to Japan. Evidently Japan's geographical propinquity is a rapidly moving affair!

First Line of Defense

The psychology of the powers in the Nineteenth Century was that war was a necessity and so "in time of peace, prepare for war." It was, therefore, highly desirable to have the first line of defense in the territory of another country. This rationalization forms a vicious circle with the doctrine of geographical propinquity. The position of Japan proper, a series of islands, is as impregnable as that of England. No power has ever threatened her independence from the Asiatic Continent. After she annexed Korea she had to concern herself with her first line of defense in Manchuria. Now that she has occupied Manchuria she considers the Siberian border and the Great Wall as her first lines of defense. Eugene O'Neill, in his "Marco's Millions," dramatizes Kublai Khan, the greatest conqueror in history. When the great Khan asked Marco Polo, how could he maintain peace throughout his realm, the Venetian replied, "Conquer everybody else in the world."

Self-Defense

It is not necessary to discuss Japan's much used but already "exploded" excuse of self-defense. The Japanese Delegate to the League of Nations, Mr. Sato, attempted to explain to the Assembly on March 4, 1932, that Japan's actions in Shanghai were those of self-defense. For the first time in history, the official representative of a great power was greeted with an outburst of sarcastic laughter by the delegates from other countries in a formal international convention.

At the time of writing there are about 100,000 Japanese troops in Chinese territory (in Manchuria and around Shanghai) and not a single Chinese soldier in Japanese territory.

The "Right" of Intervention

Japanese officials and publicists condone and even justify the Japanese wanton use of force in China on the ground that other powers had taken similar actions in the past. They have even attempted to draw parallels between the actions of their government and those of the United States in Mexico and South America. This is a tortuous as well as dangerous line of reasoning. In the first place, the actions of Japan must be judged on their own merits and according to their specific background and circumstances. In the second place, times have changed and much progress has been made in international law and ethics. There was a time when there was no international law and ethics to guide relations between nations and might did make right. It was in 1928, hardly four years ago, that the nations of the world solemnly denounced war as an instrument of national policy. What a dangerous doctrine it is to justify actions of the present by the standards of the past which have been outgrown and ⌐iscarded. If the United States were to pursue the course of Japan in collecting public and private loans, she would have to occupy most of South America, and almost all the countries in Europe!

In advancing this line of argument, Japan is also attempting to appeal to the selfish side of certain European powers whose past records in China are not at all beyond reproach, and whose vested interests placed them more or less "in the same boat" with Japan. It is apparent that Japanese diplomacy has been directed towards lining up certain European powers on Japan's side against the United States whose record in China is absolutely clean and whose intentions have always been clear. This line of attack so far has been moderately successful. Since the Council of the League of Nations convened in Paris in November 1931, France and Great Britain have toned down their attitude towards upholding the League Covenant. The newly appointed Foreign Minister of Great Britain, Sir John Simon, often referred to Japan as "our former ally," while the French press has considered Japan to be a champion of the sanctity of treaties. If Japan should succeed in aligning Great Britain and France with herself to form a *bloc* to revive the old game of mutually maintaining special interests and spheres of influence, the political situation in the Far East would revert to that dangerous state which existed at the close of the last century when John Hay declared the Open Door principle.

The Sanctity of Treaties

There are treaties and treaties as there are laws and laws. Some treaties are unjust and are imposed upon a small or weak nation by force, and some are voluntarily entered into by free and equal powers. To the former belong the "1915 Agreements" and to the latter the League of Nations Covenant, Nine Power Treaty and the Pact of Paris. Japan seems to be deeply concerned that China should observe to the letter of law the unjust treaties of dubious validity which

Japan imposed upon China at the point of a gun yet she herself flagrantly violates all three international treaties she freely and solemnly pledged herself to uphold.

How Japan "Saves"

What aggressors have not committed their acts of aggression in the name of self-defense, and what malefactors have not exploited their victims in the name of benevolence? Japan "saved" Manchuria once in 1905, "saved" Korea in 1910, and has recently "saved" Manchuria once more for the good of the people. Strange to say the Koreans and Chinese have been very "ungrateful." The following is a conclusive proof of how much Japan cares for the welfare of the Chinese people. (See Appendix VIII for the case of Korea.)

In Japan proper, the use and sale of opium and narcotics for other than medicinal purposes are prohibited by law under most severe penalties. In Formosa, a colony of the Japanese Empire, theoretically the same law applies but actually the Government Monopoly sells opium to registered addicts and closes one eye on narcotic smuggling. The government is supposed to cure the addicts within a certain time limit. However, according to the report of the Opium Research Committee of the Foreign Policy Association, the list of government-registered addicts in Formosa has never been closed.

"The opium policy pursued by the Japanese government in the Kwantung Leased Territory and the Japanese settlement in Manchuria, is directly contrary to that of the Chinese government and the Japanese government is therefore, violating Article 17 of the Hague International Opium Convention of 1912" according to a special report dated January, 1930, published by the National Anti-Opium Association of China. Throughout the Japanese leased territory and especially in Dairen, opium smoking is free not only in the government opium dens but also in restaurants and brothels.

"Now to turn to the narcotic situation in Manchuria and China proper, no less than seventy-five per cent of the Japanese nationals residing in South Manchuria are directly or indirectly connected with drug traffic, according to the estimate of Mr. U. Kikuchi, Secretary of the Association for the Prevention of Opium Evils of Japan. According to statistics issued by the Shanghai Customs authorities, for the past two years, beginning January 30, 1929, and ending April 6, 1931 a total of 80,132 ounces of opium had been discovered in forty-one Japanese steamers passing Shanghai and these huge shipments were believed to aim at Dairen as the final destination. Immediately after the Japanese occupation of Manchuria the first thing they did was the establishment of opium monopoly in the territories under their military rule, a repetition of this insidious form of conquest which she has applied to the island of Formosa and actually bore fruit."

"In Mukden, Changchun, Tsinan, Tientsin, Amoy, Foochow, etc., numerous "dope" huts are operated under Japanese consular protection in open defiance of Chinese suppression Acts. In the Japanese concession in Mukden, these huts number some two hundred the owners of which pay regular cumshas to the Japanese police in return for protection. Some one hundred morphine shops are also found to exist and these are situated either in the neighborhood of Japanese dispensaries or in the rear of Japanese residences. In a single shop, about forty to fifty persons come to receive injections per day.

"In Changchun, the condition is even worse, and opium dens reach the startling number of approximately one thousand five hundred, and are operated by Koreans, Japanese and naturalized Japanese."

According to Assessor Lyall's statements recorded in the minutes of Eleventh Session of the Advisory Committee on Traffic in Opium held in Geneva in April, 1928, "Every ounce of morphine that was smuggled into China came from Europe and Japan. In Japanese-controlled Port Arthur the annual output of the morphine factory is 700,000 lbs. or more than 30 tons.

The scope of the problem is partly indicated by the Japanese government report for 1929:

Yen

Gross revenue from sale of opium 30,277,000
Net revenue from sale of opium 20,015,196

Number of opium addicts in Kwantung, Japanese leased territory:

Year	No. of Addicts
1923	27,154
1924	28,252
1925	29,521
1926	29,172
1927	31,061

These statistics include registered addicts only.

That the Japanese government attempts to make its own people believe that Japan is the "Redeemer of China" is shown in the letter dated Feb. 8, 1932, communicated to the League of Nations Assembly from Dr. Sherwood Eddy, internationally known American Y. M. C. A. worker:

The ruthless military offensive of Japan in Manchuria and down the east coast have pierced China's heart, awakening her people to the realization of their desperate need . . .

Just before we sailed for home we witnessed the beginning of the trouble which led to the bombing of Shanghai and to the battles which are now in progress. At the invitation of the Japanese, we visited Japan for three days, had a series of interviews and met groups of representative people for discussion. We found here such a tense war-time psychology and tight censorship of press and platform that no single man in all Japan dare speak out boldly in criticism of the military adventure of army and government. Instant assassination or imprisonment would follow any such spoken word under the present fascist control of militarism. Indeed, the people are not permitted to hear or know any facts that are unfavorable to Japan. In their propaganda Japan is proclaimed 'The Redeemer of China.'

The Japanese "Monroe Doctrine"

Japan has no right to claim that she should have a "Monroe Doctrine" for Asia. She has not protected the smaller and weaker nations of the Orient. On the contrary, Japan's dealings with her neighbors have been a long series of oppressions and aggressions. In 1910 she violated her solemn pledge in annexing Korea. Since 1894 Japan has taken territory from China and has repeatedly menaced the independence of China. Furthermore, in accepting the principle of the Open Door and in signing the Nine-Power Treaty,

Japan has specifically repudiated any claim to a special right
to "protect China."

The late Prof. J. W. Jenks, in an open letter to the New
York *Times* of December 19, 1913, wrote:

> With regard to the alleged analogy between China's position
> towards Japan and Mexico's position in relation to the United States,
> I should like to say just this: What is frequently referred to as the
> Asiatic Monroe Doctrine, if it were for the protection and not for
> the molestation of China, would not be, I think, unacceptable to
> Americans who desire to help maintain a lasting peace in Asia. Such
> a doctrine was, in fact, prescribed and promoted by Mr. Hay and
> Mr. Root. But the trouble is that certain Japanese who are now
> advocating what they call a Japanese Monroe Doctrine regarding
> China inject into their arguments and policies, arguments and poli-
> cies which Americans would never have applied nor would they
> now apply towards our Latin-American neighbors. China is not
> assisted toward an acceptance of Japanese intervention by Japan's
> record in Korea and in Southern Manchuria. Any extension of po-
> litical influence of this sort is naturally regarded by China as an
> assault, deliberately intended upon China's sovereignty.

"Chaotic" China

That China is going through a period of social and political re-adjustment all statesmen will recognize. The size
of the population of the country and the inertia of her long
history and tradition require sufficient time for proper
changes to take place in China. When left alone freely to
work out her own problems China will make the re-adjustments, perhaps slowly, but surely in accordance with her
background and racial genius. Every other country has
gone through a similar period. Hardly a hundred and fifty
years ago France was changed from an empire into a re-

public. It was the interference from outside into her internal affairs that made the French Revolution the most bloody and stormy event of modern Europe.

Least of all can Japan point a finger of scorn at the internal disorder in China. Recent events have shown clearly that "well-governed" Japan has not been able to control its own army and navy which have not only scrapped international treaties and the solemn pledges of their own government but also created a dangerous and intolerable situation in Manchuria. Moreover, the internal conditions of Japan are not as stable as their publicists would have the world believe. Politically, the war clique controls the Government in spite of the fact that the Liberal Party has a much larger following. The wealth of the Empire is concentrated in the hands of a few families. The appearance of stability has been maintained by the autocratic and despotic rule. The only difference between the War Lords of China and the war clique of Japan is that the former are old-fashioned and disorganized while the latter is modern and highly efficient. The former group brings suffering to the Chinese people while the latter is not only a menace to Japan but to the peace of the whole world.

Maintain "Peace and Stability"

Japan claims that the peace and stability of Manchuria are indispensable to her national existence. The Chinese people of Manchuria also want peace because they have to live there. The question is, has Japan a right to maintain peace in Chinese territory? Is it possible for a foreign power to enforce peace by military occupation?

The Japanese claim that the presence of Japanese troops and the South Manchuria Railway "zone" have been stabilizing influences. This contention does not stand analysis. Prior to September 1931, Japan controlled less than 1400 square miles, less than one-half of one per cent of the whole territory of Manchuria in which she stationed less than 15,000 troops. Since that time Japanese forces have occupied and are still occupying over 200,000 square miles of territory, with at least 35,000 troops, and yet, according to the Japanese Government, lawnessness and "bandit uprising" have since been multiplying day by day. The Japanese themselves often contradict each other on this point. On November 11, 1931, the Japanese Ambassador to France, speaking before the Anglo-American Press Association in Paris, said, in justifying Japanese occupation of Manchuria, "Speaking in a single word, we have succeeded in transforming Manchuria into a country better governed than the rest of China." The next day the Paris *Daily Mail* published a special statement by General Honjo in which he claimed emphatically that the reason why Japan was fighting in Manchuria was because of the frequent occurrence there of murder, arson and plunder. The claims of Ambassador Yoshizawa and General Honjo, as conflicting as they are, are typical of the claims put forth by Japanese officials and publicists.

Liberal leaders in Japan are not slow to realize that times have changed. Time was when strong powers did use force to maintain order in comparatively weaker countries to "protect" life, property and investments of its nationals, irrespective of what the internal situation might

mean to the country itself. Speaking before the Japanese
Diet on January 21, 1926, in opposition to the Positive Policy
of Japan in China as advocated by the followers of General Baron Tanaka, the then Japanese Minister of Foreign
Affairs, Baron Shidehara said:

> No doubt the complete tranquility of the whole region of the
> Three Eastern Provinces (Manchuria) undisturbed by any scourge
> of war is very much to be desired in the interest of the native popu-
> lation, as well as of the Japanese residents. It is, however, a responsi-
> bility that properly rests upon China. The assumption of that
> responsibility by Japan without just cause would be manifestly in-
> consistent with the fundamental conception of the existing inter-
> national relations, with the basic principle of the Washington
> treaties, and with the repeated declarations of the Japanese govern-
> ment. By taking such course we would forfeit our national honor
> and pride once for all. In no case, and by no means, can we be
> party to so improvident an action.

Professor Nitobe of Tokyo Imperial University, comments in his book entitled "Japan"—

> The harm and utter uselessness of their (the Japanese troops)
> presence in a country where they were not welcome, were made the
> subject of innumerable attacks on the Japanese Government both at
> home and abroad; but the misinformed military clique in Tokyo
> were deaf to reason. It took many months to convince them of the
> error of their ways, but not until the sum of £150,000,000 had been
> expended and hundreds of lives sacrificed, were the regiments brought
> back from Siberia in the autumn of 1922.

Is China a Nation?

In evading her obligations under the Nine Power Treaty
Japan laboriously attempts to prove that China is not a
nation and has no responsible government and that there

is no territorial integrity or administrative independence to violate. At the same time she insists on direct negotiation with the Chinese Government and holds the Chinese Government responsible for the economic boycott.

It is true China has not yet acquired all the technique, machinery and ideology of a modern state. Perhaps she does not want to duplicate western political methods. In the first place it is questionable whether a modern state is an entire success. Secondly, modern political science is not based on, and has not yet demonstrated its capacity to solve, political problems of China's magnitude.

China is about the size of Europe and has almost as large a population. Up to the recent period of re-adjustment China has achieved peace and stability to a degree unknown in Western history. Where and when in Europe or anywhere else did 400 million people govern themselves successfully and for such a long period? Not one-half or one-thrid of that number. Even when the Roman Empire at the peak of glory could not compare with the Chinese Empire, and the Roman Empire is no more.

Even during the last fifteen years conditions in China have not been much worse than those in Europe. Certainly the intersectional rivalry, heterogeneity of language and conflict of cultures and races of Europe are not comparable with the high degree of homogeneity in China.

Viewed in historical perspective, China is the most stable civilization in world history. It was only 156 years ago that the thirteen American colonies became independent. From the American Revolution to the Civil War, a period of 85 years, the young American Republic was not wholly stable.

In her history of 4000 years, China has enjoyed several periods of great prosperity. For example, in the Chou dynasty, 1200 years before the Christian era, China's civilization blossomed forth during 800 years of peace and progress. The Tang dynasty, the golden age of Chinese art and literature, extended from 618 to 907 A.D., a period of almost 300 years. The Ming dynasty (1368–1644 A.D.), famous in the West for its paintings of porcelains, covers a period of 276 years. Just before the present period of political re-adjustment and social change, China enjoyed a period of stability for over two centuries under the Ching dynasty. Any one of those periods of peace and stability is longer than the whole history of the United States. This ancient nation changed from an empire into a republic in 1911. Is it fair to expect China to settle all of her social and political problems in 21 years, while it took over 75 years for France or the United States to make her re-adjustments?

Furthermore, the transformation in China is far more complex and complicated than that confronted France or the United States. Compared with Western history it is like undergoing the Renaissance, the Industrial Revolution, the American Revolution and the Civil War all at the same time. China has developed her own way and attitude toward social change and her standards of value. She is not willing to copy and imitate without first understanding the implications of such measures. Those who would have China changed over-night into a second Japan, or America, have, of course, become impatient and cynical.

Japan is a younger nation than China. She has only known constitutional government in recent years. Up until seventy years ago, the Emperor and the Shogunate had ruled Japan by a theo-military dictatorship in the form of an absolute monarchy. The Japanese Empire had been divided into a number of feudal states until as late as 1871. The recent political change in Japan has been comparatively simple and easy because of the small size of the country and population, and especially because the change was effected by the dictatorship from the top down. On the other hand, China, in making her much more difficult and complicated readjustments, has not only twenty-five times the area of Japan proper and seven times the Japanese population, but also the tradition and attitude evolved through the centuries of political *laissez faire* and individualism, which makes it necessary for changes to be brought about from the bottom up.

During recent years the achievements of Japan have been phenomenal. In certain things she deserves universal admiration, such as in the fields of science and research in Chinese art and classics. But China has not been impressed by Japan's social and political life as a whole because it is not yet authentic and mature. Her apparent modernization hides a sad and tragic interior. She understands neither China nor the New World.

It is extremely unfortunate that in adopting the outward forms of Chinese culture and civilization in the former days, Japan did not adopt also China's tolerance and love of peace, and that in imitating the West more recently, she has not advanced with the West and has not outgrown the ideas and methods of jingoism and imperialism of the Nineteenth Century.

APPENDIX TO CHAPTER XVI

PERIODS OF IMPORTANT CHINESE DYNASTIES

		Period	*Duration*
Hsia	B.C.	2205–1765	440 years
Shang (or Yin)	"	1766–1121	645 "
Chou	"	1122– 224	898 "
Ch'in	"	225– 205	20 "
Han	"	206–A.D. 25	231 "
The Three Kingdom Period	A.D.	26– 264	238 "
Chin	"	265– 317	52 "
Period of North and South	"	318– 557	239 "
Sui	"	589– 617	28 "
Tang	"	618– 906	288 "
Five Dynasties	"	907– 959	52 "
Sung	"	960–1279	319 "
Yuan	"	1280–1367	87 "
Ming	"	1368–1643	275 "
Ching	"	1644–1911	267 "
The Republic	"	1912–	

CHAPTER XVII

MILITARISM AND THE SCHOLASTIC EMPIRE

Similarities and Contrasts between China and Japan

GENERALLY speaking, China and Japan are both oriental countries. The latter has inherited from China much of her genuine culture and civilization. Even today, Chinese art, classics, and philosophy form the essential part of learning in Japan. For centuries there has existed a strong cultural bond between the learned men of the two countries. Professor Inazo Nitobe of the Imperial University of Tokyo writes in his book on "Japanese Traits and Foreign Influences":

China had the oldest and most advanced civilization. Korea throve under her intellectual and political guidance. Later, the Koreans passed on their imported arts and sciences to Japan, when she was just emerging from the bronze age.

. . . . .

The cultural penetrations of China—for other kinds of penetration in any period of Japanese history we have no trace—was in full swing as early as the fourth century A.D., China being then under the rule of the famous Tang Dynasty. In art and literature, in philosophy and law, in administration and handicrafts, Chinese lessons and precepts proved to be the most powerful moulding influences. These were exercised without compulsion of any kind. It was an instance of an intrinsically higher culture benignantly and automatically flowing into the needy lower levels.

134

Although similar in culture, China and Japan furnish most striking contrasts in their political backgrounds.

On Emperor Worship

China has long outgrown the doctrine of divine right of kings. Fifteen hundred years before the founding of Rome, the Chinese people had already the doctrine of the "Mandate of Heaven." In Shu-King, one of the oldest Chinese writings, the "Mandate of Heaven" was defined as "Heaven sees as the people see and Heaven hears as the people hear." This early tradition was elaborated upon by Mencius who lived in the 4th Century B.C. Mencius taught that in a nation the most important consideration is the welfare of the people. The government and the rituals come next, while the monarch occupies third place. As long as the ruler obeys the Mandate of Heaven and treats the people as if they are his children, the people should be as devoted and loyal to him as if he were their parent; but as soon as the ruler disobeys the "Mandate of Heaven" and considers the people as if they are dust and grass, then the people have the inherent right of overthrowing him and setting up a benevolent monarch.

During the history of China, the Chinese people have by popular uprisings set up and overthrown more than twenty-six dynasties and ruling families.

Japan, on the other hand, has had the same ruling family since the beginning of her history, and the Japanese people still worship the Emperor as divine.

Attitude Toward the Soldier

Toward the end of the Chou dynasty (1122–224 B.C.), China was divided into several feudal states warring against one another for supremacy. The conditions existing at that time resemble those prevalent in modern Europe. There was national rivalry and jealousy which led to secret diplomacy and entangling alliances. Competitive armament vied with protective tariff. Regulations governing the admission of aliens were almost as elaborate as present day immigration laws. There was so much inter-state warfare that warriors and strategists became the ruling class in all the feudal states. Those conditions compelled the philosophers and teachers of that time to turn their attention to problems of international order and peace.

The three outstanding philosophers who have influenced the thinking of the Chinese people throughout the ages are Confucius, Mencius, and Mo-Tze. All three advocated benevolence or virtue as the ideal and most effective principle of social control, and all three indicted in no uncertain terms the use of force as the most undesirable way of settling domestic and international problems. When Confucius edited the Annals of Spring and Autumn (the history of the Chou dynasty), he recognized no righteous wars. Mencius contrasted *Jen* (benevolence or virtue), with *Pah* (the use of force), as two principles of government and international relations. "The people willingly and intelligently follow the rule by *Jen* and therefore their allegiance is permanent and from the desire of the heart. *Pah* compels obedience and therefore the allegiance of the people is based on fear, and is temporary." "In an ideal international order the more benevolent and virtuous nations will be voluntarily followed by the less benevolent and virtuous. The most chaotic conditions will prevail when the more powerful nations attempt to dominate and swallow up the smaller and weaker nations." Mo-Tze was perhaps the most explicit in his teachings on international relations. He advocated three great doctrines: *Fei-Kung* (non-aggression); *Mi-Ping* (abolition of soldiery); and *Chien-Ai* (inclusive love). Mo-Tze was against all forms of aggression, military as well as economic. He specifically advocated the abolition of war and of competitive armaments in his doctrine of abolition of soldiery. He said that the human race had advanced to the state of civilization where society ostracized and punished the murderer of one life. Mankind must advance to a higher state of civilization where it would also ostracize and punish the murderer of many lives. This philosopher did not think that people could carry out non-aggression and abolition of soldiery until they learned the doctrine of inclusive love, by which they respect other people's rights and personality as if they were their own.

The teachings of these three philosophers exerted great influence upon the Chinese people. Consequently, the Chinese Empire evolved into what is called by western scholars a "Scholastic Empire" ruled by an intellectual aristocracy.

The Chinese people have acquired for centuries a veneration for the learned man and a dislike for the soldier. In social esteem the scholar is at the top and the soldier at

the bottom of the social ladder. Chinese historians have
not glorified wars and warriors.

In Japan, the warriors have always been the ruling class.
The Samurai tradition still prevails, and the war clique is
the modern counterpart of the Shogunate. Even today, the
military branch of the Japanese government is not subject
to the civilian branch, but is responsible only to the Emperor who is above the constitution.

Japanese Military Clique Makes Desperate Stand

When the Liberal Party was in power in Japan from the
Washington Conference to 1927, disputes between China
and Japan were usually adjusted by conciliatory methods.
The war clique is opposed to the Liberal Party, and its attitude toward Manchuria is based upon the following points:
(1), Japan deserves to own Manchuria because she sacrificed
so much money and so many lives in the Russo-Japanese
War; (2), the resources of Manchuria are necessary to enable Japan to become the dominating economic power in
the Pacific; (3, Japan is destined to establish an empire
on the Asiatic continent.

Since the Washington Conference of 1922 liberal sentiment and the Liberal Party have been growing in Japan.
In the meantime, substantial progress has been made in
developing peace sentiment and peace machinery throughout the world. All this the Japanese Military Clique considers a menace to its very existence, because war will be
stripped of its former glory and be increasingly considered
undesirable. Furthermore, the masses of the Japanese

people have begun to realize their power. Depression and unemployment have brought about great discontent among the farmers and workers. The war clique, in whose hands is concentrated the political power of the Empire, has viewed these trends with apprehension, and has been planning to strengthen its position by an imperialistic adventure which may also serve to divert the attention of the masses from their own plight. In invading Manchuria, the militarists of Japan have decided to make a last desperate stand.

Last autumn the rest of the world was preoccupied with a most serious economic depression, and China, in addition to her problems of political and economic reconstruction, has been paralyzed with the worst floods in her history. The militarists of Japan decided that it was the opportune time to strike. Grover Clark, for many years a resident in and a student of Japan and China, said in an address before the Massachusetts League of Women Voters on January 26, 1932:

Why did Japan's military do this? I say Japan's 'Military' advisedly because the responsibility for the original move in Manchuria rests squarely on the military faction in Japan, not on the people of the country nor on the civilian leaders in the government, however much these latter may share in the responsibility for the subsequent Japanese military expansion. On the basis of considerable knowledge of the situation in Japan as well as in Manchuria, and of the attitude of both the Japanese military leaders and the Japanese civilian officials in Japan and Manchuria, I am convinced that the chief motive of the military was to regain power in Japan itself.

Formerly they dominated the country. In recent years their power has been decreasing. On several occasions they have tried to create a situation in China which would lead to a wave of nationalistic feeling in Japan, so that they might ride back into power on the crest of that wave. They tried to do this without success in 1927 and 1928, in their moves in Shantung. They began, in 1931, to stir up feeling in Japan at the end of June. They moved in Manchuria in September suddenly and, as the evidence clearly shows, after careful preparation. They hoped to arouse so much feeling in Japan that the civilian authorities would be helpless. They succeeded. They have secured complete control.

China Followed a Different Direction

As late as the beginning of the Nineteenth Century, China was still a loose confederation of autonomous communities, based on the principle that a government is best when it governs the least. It did not have a competitive system of business and industry. It had not developed a modern army and navy with modern implements of war. Above all, it did not have the modern spirit of nationalism.

The first Chinese who ever received Western education was Yung Wing, who graduated from Yale University in 1854. Upon his return to China, he immediately saw two great needs of his country—modern guns and modern education. True to her background, the Chinese people have taken to modern education much more readily than to modern guns. Consequently China has made steady progress in modern education, while her armament today is at least one century behind.

The ignorant "war-lords" of China—and the Chinese people do know what a curse they have been to China —have never been respected by the people. Their number is decreasing rapidly. They have only acquired power within the last twenty years, and will not remain in power much longer. At their worst they bring suffering upon the Chinese people. But the army generals and admirals are still venerated by the Japanese people and they exercise great power in the government. During the recent crisis it has been clearly demonstrated that they are no less unruly than the Chinese "war-lords." With a highly equipped fighting machine and the misled support of the masses of Japan, is not the Japanese war clique not only a menace to Japan herself but also to the whole world?

The Nineteenth Route Army Symbolic of the Nation

What the Nineteenth Route Army of China has done at Chapei and Woosung is now a chapter of history. Those brave defenders of Shanghai have already joined the company of martyrs and immortals.

To China the resistance by the Nineteenth Route Army has become a national inspiration and symbol. An inspiration because, since the Opium War almost a century ago, this is the first army that has effectively resisted a great military power and undone the myth of the "invincible" army. A well-known British writer had characterized China as "a nation accustomed to defeat and humiliation at the hands of foreign armed forces." In spite of its poor equipment, insufficient ammunition, and without any military airplanes, the Nineteenth Route Army stood its ground under aerial and artillery bombardments that "surpassed the Great War in intensity and destruction." According to eye-witnesses, on March 3, 1932, the defenders of Woosung when surrounded refused to surrender, but fought to the end, shouting,

"Chung-Hua-Min-Kuo-Wan-Sui—Long live the Republic of China!"

While the defenders were fighting against great odds at Chapei and Woosung, the youths throughout the country volunteered for military training. In several instances, the students had to compel the school authorities to employ army instructors. In Shanghai women students volunteered for Red Cross service in such large numbers that many were turned away weeping because they could not do their share to defend their country. Never before had the rising generation of China realized the necessity of preparedness.

Western observers have named Woosung the Chinese "Verdun." The Nineteenth Route Army has erected there a monument that is symbolic, not only of China's determination to resist foreign invasions, but also of China's traditional attitude toward militarism: "They shall not pass!"

CHAPTER XVIII

THE UNITED STATES AND NEW DIPLOMACY

The Open Door

FROM 1842, when China was forcibly opened to the West by the Opium War, to 1898, the great powers were scrambling for concessions and settlements in China. Great Britain had obtained ports in Shantung and the harbor of Hongkong; France in southern China; Germany in Eastern Shantung; and Russia in Manchuria and Mongolia, while Japan, a comparatively late comer, claimed Fukien as her sphere of influence. China was threatened with partition. International rivalry and jealousy were leading toward a worldwide conflict.

Secretary of State, John Hay, of the United States, seeing the imminent danger to China and world peace, sent two different notes in September and November 1899 to Great Britain, France, Germany, Russia, Italy, and Japan. Setting forth the principle of equal opportunity for all nations to trade in China, which became known later as the Open Door Policy, the necessary implication of the declaration was the preservation of the independence of China. Thus John Hay re-affirmed officially and definitely the policy which the United States had followed from the beginning of her contact with the Far East in 1784, over a century before. It is significant that in 1900, when the Boxer Uprising was at its worst, Secretary of State Hay sent a circular telegram to eleven powers, on July 3rd, stating more explicitly the Open Door principle.

In this critical posture of affairs in China it is deemed appropriate to define the attitude of the United States. . . . We adhere to the policy initiated by us in 1857 of peace with the Chinese nation, of furtherance of lawful commerce, and of protection of lives and property of our citizens. . . . The purpose of the President is, as it has been heretofore, to act concurrently with the other powers . . . the policy of the . . . United States is to seek a solution which may bring about permanent safety and peace to China, preserve Chinese territorial and administrative entity, protect all rights guaranteed to friendly powers by treaty and international law, and safeguard for the world the principle of equal and impartial trade with all parts of the Chinese Empire.

The Open Door is undoubtedly a monumental document of American statesmanship, next to the Declaration of Independence in its international import. It is a forerunner of the League of Nations Covenant and the Briand-Kellogg Pact.

Some writers are inclined to think that perhaps Hay had in mind primarily American trade interests in the Far East. Perhaps so, but the trade of the United States with China was negligible at that time. It is difficult to believe that trade was the chief concern of the Open Door.

Since that time, the United States has consistently adhered to this principle. Though Russia gained control of the Chinese Eastern Railway and extended illegally its jurisdiction over Chinese territory, the American government has refused to recognize such rights acquired by Russia and later claimed by Japan.

The United States and the "1915 Agreements"

In 1915 the United States Government, commenting on the implications of the Twenty-One Demands, sent the following identical note to China and Japan:

> In view of the circumstances of the negotiations which have taken place and which are now pending between the Government of China and the Government of Japan and of the agreements which have been reached as a result thereof, the Government of the United States has the honor to notify the Government of the Chinese Republic that it cannot recognize any agreement or undertaking which has been entered into or which may be entered into between the Governments of China and Japan impairing the rights of the United States and its citizens in China, the political or territorial integrity of the Republic of China, or the international policy relative to China, commonly known as the Open Door Policy.

Japan's Occupation of Siberia

In 1918 the Allies sent an international expeditionary force to Siberia. While England and the United States each sent 7,000 troops, Japan at first declared that she would send 17,000 troops, but 70,000 she finally sent. Not long after the armistice, other powers withdrew their forces, but Japan refused to do so and did not withdraw until four years later.

Disturbed by the prolonged occupation of a section of Siberia by Japan, the United States addressed the following note to the Japanese Government:

> In view of its conviction that the course followed by the Government of Japan brings into question the very definite understanding concluded at the time troops were sent to Siberia, the Government of the United States must in candor explain its position and say to

the Japanese Government that the Government of the United States can neither now or hereafter recognize as valid any claims or titles out of the present occupation and control, and that it can not acquiesce in any action taken by the Government of Japan which might impair existing treaty rights or the political or territorial integrity of Russia. (Made public in the Statement of the United States at the Washington Conference, 1921–22.)

Although China is the largest potential market for the United States, American trade with Japan is as yet much more important than that with China. Throughout the present crisis, Secretary of State Stimson has acted, it would seem, without the consideration of self-interest. At the very beginning he sounded the note that is prophetic of the new era of diplomacy as illustrated by the following extracts from the correspondence on the Manchurian question which President Hoover transmitted to the United States Senate on January 27, 1932:

This situation is of concern morally, legally and politically to a considerable number of nations. It is not exclusively a matter of concern to Japan and China. —Secretary Stimson to Baron Debuchi on Sept. 22, 1931.

The Secretary of State cannot understand how the bombing of Chinchow can be minimized or how it can be said to be of no importance. The explanation given by the Japanese military authorities seems quite inadequate. —Secretary Stimson to Baron Shidehara on Oct. 11, 1931.

A threat of war, wherever it may arise, is of profound concern to the whole world, and for this reason the American Government, like other governments, was constrained to call to the attention of both disputants the serious dangers involved in the present situation. —Secretary Stimson's note of Oct. 20, 1931, to China and Japan calling attention to the obligations of the Kellogg-Briand Pact.

My government cannot escape the conclusion that in the efforts to protect the South Manchuria Railway—a situation has been created in Manchuria which gives Japan substantial control of South Manchuria and has, temporarily at least, destroyed the administrative integrity of China in this region. —Ambassador Forbes to Japan, Nov. 5, 1931.

The American Government . . . cannot admit the legality of any situation de facto nor does it intend to recognize any treaty or agreement . . . which may impair the treaty rights of the United States or its citizens in China. —Secretary Stimson's identic note of Jan. 7, 1932, to China and Japan.

In Japan's reply dated January 16, 1932, to Secretary of State Stimson's note of January 7, 1932, the Japanese Government stated "it might be the subject of an academic doubt whether, in a given case, the impropriety of the means necessarily and always voids the ends secured," is typical of all cynics towards the new diplomacy and the new international order.

Japan has repeatedly pointed to the slowness with which China readjusts her social and political interests in condonation of her aggressions on China. In contrast to this, the United States government pioneered to a new height of international magnanimity when Secretary of State Stimson wrote in his letter to Senator Borah, dated Feb. 24, 1932:

At the time this treaty (the Nine Power Treaty) was signed, it was known that China was engaged in an attempt to develop the free institutions of a self-governing republic after her recent evolution from an autocratic form of government; that she would require many years of both economic and political effort to that end, that her progress would necessarily be slow.

The course taken by the United States during the crisis has reassured the Chinese people and strengthened the traditional friendship between the two countries. Nor is this new idealistic diplomacy incompatible with realistic interests. On the contrary, good-will and confidence is the foundation of trade, and American businessmen are the first to recognize this truth. China, with her huge population and vast territory and not yet developed industrially, is the largest potential market in the world. It would require a miracle now to persuade the Chinese people to trade with Japan. Japanese publicists have attempted to create an impression in this country that the best way to invest in China is through Japanese firms. As an American observer pointed out, "Anyone who thinks he can safely invest his money, either in Manchuria or in Japan, as long as Japan is committed to the project of pacifying Manchuria, is an incredible optimist, in view of the history of the world in recent years." According to the American National Foreign Trade Council, while Japanese exports to China dropped considerably last year, the United States exports to China increased in spite of the unfavorable exchange caused by the unprecedented decline in the value of silver.

Those Belligerent Chinese!

—From *The San Francisco Chronicle.*

CHAPTER XIX

THE CRISIS AND WORLD PEACE

MENG TZE, or Mencius, foremost Chinese political philosopher, once said, "The difference between a man and a beast is not very great." He went on to explain that the physical structure and desires of both are essentially the same. That which definitely differentiates a man from a beast is that man has learned to use his intellect and to appreciate spiritual values. In the use of physical force, a beast is often superior to man.

This is human progress in a nutshell. Primitive man was not much different from a beast. Even thousands of years after he came out of the cave, he still insisted on using force to settle disputes. Now individual disputes are settled on the basis of law and equity.

The tragic thing is that group behavior, or mob psychology, always lags behind individual behavior. Many years after law courts were established for individuals, nations still used war to settle disputes.

The Great War taught mankind the lesson that war settles nothing, but, instead, creates worse problems. Thinkers and statesmen have since then built up peace sentiment and peace machinery, which will help nations to settle disputes by peaceful means.

The substance of the disputes is a separate question from how disputes should be settled.

Both China and Japan are pledged under the League of Nations Covenant and the Pact of Paris to settle disputes by peaceful means.

In Part I it has been shown that there is conflict between China and Japan. The fundamental interests of the Chinese and Japanese people are not necessarily opposed, but the political and military policy of the Japanese Empire comes into conflict with those of China. Treaties have been concluded; some have been recognized by China and some have not. Some of the treaties are one-sided and unjust, and some were forced upon China at the point of a gun.

The gist of the Manchurian problem is that Japan needs the agricultural products of Manchuria. From the point of view of a possible war with China, Russia or with some other power, Japan needs also iron and coal and a base for military operations on the Asiatic continent. China has been weak politically and militarily. Therefore, Japan has taken advantage of the internal situation in China to dominate Manchuria. This conflict all the time leads to disputes over treaties, treaty-interpretations, and local clashes. On one hand, Japan claims a long list of treaty violations and unsettled cases. On the other hand, China believes that some alleged treaties are unjust and some are not treaties at all, while some treaties are being interpreted by Japan to her advantage without valid grounds.

Direct Negotiations Unfair

That there are outstanding disputes between China and Japan no one will deny. The question is how to settle these disputes. Direct negotiation offers a way out if no force is used by one of the parties. This has not been the case with Japan. Even in minor cases, Japan has usually applied military pressure to bring China to terms. The Twenty-One Demands is the most infamous, but nevertheless typical of Japanese methods. More often than not Japan has usually attached political conditions of a serious nature to minor cases in direct negotiations. The following is a typical case reported by W. W. Willoughby in his standard works, "Foreign Rights and Interests in China":

Chengchiatun Incident and Resulting Japanese Demands

In September, 1916, there came a further official exposition of the desires and intentions of the Japanese Government pressed upon China because of an alleged wrong done to its nationals in a fracas which arose in January, 1916, between Chinese and Japanese soldiers in the small town of Chengchiatun, near the border of Mongolia.

The evidence as to what occurred at that time is conflicting, but, so far as it can be reduced to a definite and credible basis it would appear that the Japanese soldiers were the aggressors and, in fact, in the wrong throughout the trouble. And, in this connection, it may be observed that Japan had no treaty or other legal right to have soldiers at Chengchiatun at all. For the purposes of this volume, however, the important fact is as to the demands which Japan predicated upon this event. These, in addition to the requirements that the general commanding the local Chinese division of troops should be punished, the officers concerned dismissed, and all who took a direct part in the fracas punished, included the demand that China should agree "to the stationing of Japanese police officers in places in South Manchuria and Eastern Inner Mongolia where their presence was considered necessary for the protection of Japanese subjects. China also to agree to the engagement by the officials of South Manchuria of Japanese police advisers." In other words, that Japan should be given an indefinite and therefore general right to participate in the policing of whatever portions of South Manchuria and Eastern Inner Mongolia she might think desirable.

But this was not all. The following "desiderata" were also presented:

1. Chinese troops stationed in South Manchuria and Eastern Inner Mongolia to employ a certain number of Japanese military officers as advisers.

2. Chinese Military Cadet Schools to employ a certain number of Japanese military officers as instructors.

3. The Military Governor of Mukden to proceed personally to Port Arthur to the Japanese Military Governor of Kwantung to apologize for the occurrence and to tender similar apologies to the Japanese Consul General in Mukden.

4. Adequate compensations to be paid by China to the Japanese sufferers and to the families of those killed.

These demands and desiderata, it is to be observed, were based upon facts as alleged by the Japanese and not as determined by any thorough or bilateral examination as to who had been in the wrong."

After Japan occupied South Manchuria, she attempted to prevent China from invoking the assistance of the League of Nations. When the League Council requested her to withdraw her troops from Chinese territory, she insisted on direct negotiation to settle fundamental principles before withdrawal, and yet she refused to define those principles. Direct negotiation with Japanese troops on Chinese soil is like talking terms between two men, one holding the other by his throat. If Japan had just claims she should have welcomed impartial investigation and arbitration.

The Existing Peace Machinery

There are four international instrumentalities for peaceful settlement—The League of Nations Covenant, the Per-

manent Court of International Justice, the Nine-Powers
Treaty, and the Pact of Paris. The Pact of Paris is the latest
and most inclusive treaty under which about sixty nations
including Japan have pledged themselves that "the settlement or solution of all disputes or conflicts of whatever
nature, or of whatever origin they may be, which may arise
among them shall never be sought except by pacific means."
It goes a step further than the League Covenant in its renunciation of all wars and in that its adherents include
Russia and the United States who are not members of the
League. But so far no machinery has been set up under
the Pact so that some procedure or steps could be taken to
prevent one of the signatories from violating the Pact. Its
greatest value is the moral renunciation that, for the first
time in international law, stripped war of its legality and
respectability.

The Permanent Court is essential a judicial body that
renders legal opinions on international disputes. The parties that refer their disputes to the Court abide by its decision because the prestige of this group of internationally
prominent jurists invariably carries great weight on the
question under consideration. However, its jurisdiction is
not compulsory, excepting over those nations which have
accepted the so-called "optional clause." Japan has not
accepted the optional clause which was accepted by 48 states
including China.

The Nine Power Treaty provides that "whenever a
situation arises which in the opinion of any one of them
involves the application of the stipulations of the present
treaty, and renders desirable discussion of such application,

there shall be full and frank communication between the contracting parties concerned."

In the present crisis, Japan had not discussed the situation with the other signatories before she took action. The treaty itself, unfortunately, does not provide any procedure or sanction by which the stipulations of the treaty may be enforced.

It is significant to point out in this connection that while most states have concluded many bilateral arbitration treaties, Japan has concluded none except one with Switzerland and even then with a number of reservations that tend to annul the effectiveness of the treaty.

The League of Nations is established for the purpose, among other things, of settling disputes among its members. Fifty-five powers, including China and Japan, have accepted the obligations of the Covenant. Article XI of the Covenant provides that any war or threat of war shall be a matter of concern to the League. If the dispute is "likely to lead to a rupture" the members pledge themselves to submit to the Council or Assembly their case for investigation and arbitration under Article XV. The parties to the dispute agree that they will not go to war with a party which accepts the unanimous decision of the Council or Assembly, not including the disputants. If any party violates this undertaking, Article XVI makes the culprit *"ipso facto* be deemed to have committed an act of war against all other members of the League" which shall enforce their wish by an economic boycott, or, if found necessary, by military means.

China and Japan and the League

Since the League of Nations was the only peace machinery available, China appealed immediately to the League in accordance with Article XI of the Covenant.

Her position from the very beginning has been to abide by the decision of the Council.

Dr. Sze, the Chinese delegate, in informing the Council on October 23, 1931, that the Chinese Government was prepared to accept the resolution, did so in a statement from which the following extracts may be quoted:

The Chinese Government accepts this proposal and declares its readiness to carry out to the full all the obligations it lays upon China. Not only does my Government accept, it is willing to go further and to do everything possible to dissipate the apprehensions of the Japanese representative with regard to the safety of Japanese lives and property in the areas re-occupied by the Chinese authorities. I believe these apprehensions to be entirely unfounded. In the view of the Chinese Government, the insecurity and disorder that have arisen within the area occupied by the Japanese troops have their origin precisely in the Japanese occupation, will grow the longer the occupation continues, and will disappear with its termination. But I wish to state that I owe it to courtesy to declare that I am convinced the Japanese Government's anxiety is genuine, and I would ask my Japanese colleague in return to believe that the Chinese Government is sincerely desirous to remove any possible apprehensions on this score.

So strong is this desire, indeed, that not only do I accept the proposal in the resolution to invite neutral officers, but I am prepared to go further and to assure the Japanese representatives and other Members of the Council that the Chinese Government is willing to examine in the most conciliatory spirit here and now any proposals for extending the system of neutral officers or, with the help of the League, devising any other arrangements on the spot to guarantee the safety of Japanese lives and property in the re-occupied territory, in order to dispel any apprehensions the Japanese Government may entertain as to the danger to its subjects that might result from compliance with the Council's resolution.

Now I come to one more point, which the Chinese Government regards as crucial. Paragraph 6 of the Resolution before us makes it clear that withdrawal is the only subject before the Council at present and that, until withdrawal has been completed, no other issue arises. But I should like to make it quite plain that, in the view of the Chinese Government, the only immediate issue arising out of the present situation besides withdrawal is the question of responsibility and assessing damages for the events that have occurred since September 18th. The Chinese Government is willing—nay, anxious, and has been from the beginning—to submit to any form of neutral third-party judgment on this issue, in accordance with the League principles and precedents and in conformity with elementary justice.

Any attempt to make the military invasion of Manchuria the occasion for pressing the solution of other claims would be contrary to the spirit of the Covenant and a violation of Article 2 of the Pact of Paris. China will not discuss any subject with any Power under the pressure of military occupation of her territory, nor what amounts to the same thing, under the pressure of accomplished fact resulting from the use of force during such occupation. The point is vital and goes to the root of the whole controversy before the Council; it is, indeed, the basic principle on which the Covenant and the Pact of Paris are founded. It is because, in the view of the Chinese Government, this point is vital and fundamental that I have stressed it, and it is for the same reason I add that the Chinese Government is assured that, in adopting this attitude, it has, as a matter of course, the full and unqualified moral support of every Member of the League and signatory of the Pact of Paris.

It further goes without saying that any discussion between China and any other Power on any subject must take place on the basis of China's rights and obligations under the Covenant and Pact of Paris, and must respect the principles laid down at the Washington Conference of 1922 with regard to the relations between China and other Powers.

In this connection, I wish to say very clearly and deliberately that, once this unhappy incident is settled and normal relations restored between China and Japan, the Japanese Government will find us not only willing, but also anxious, to discuss every issue between the two countries in the most friendly spirit. China has but one desire—to live at peace with all countries and particularly so with her neighbors, and hopes that the very magnitude of the shock to the relations of the two countries that has brought them before the League will result in the stubborn resolve on both sides to put these relations on a new and better footing and to lay the foundation for permanent peace in the Far East. It is in this spirit that the Chinese Government welcomes the Council's proposal of a permanent conciliation commission, or similar body, and it is in this spirit, too, that I wish to assure the Council that the Chinese Government for its part, will not only scrupulously observe all its obligations under international law and practice to promote good relations with Japan, but will do every thing in its power to turn the thoughts of its people to peace and amity, forgetfulness of the bitter past, and hope for a better future.

On October 26, 1931, China declared once more to the Council:

China, like every member of the League of Nations, bound by the Covenant to 'a scrupulous respect for all treaty obligations.' The Chinese Government for its part is determined loyally to fulfil all its obligations under the Covenant. It is prepared to give proofs of this intention by undertaking to settle all disputes with Japan as to treaty interpretation by arbitration or judicial settlement, as provided in Article 13 of the Covenant.

Throughout the Council meetings Japan has insisted on direct negotiation on political issues before withdrawal of troops, and yet, of late, has asserted that there is no responsible government in China, and, therefore, that she has not violated the administrative integrity of China. Furthermore, she insists that Chinese troops in Chinese territory in the vicinity of the invading forces constitute a menace. Japan has arrogated to herself the right to drive Chinese troops as far back as she deems desirable. She has even bombarded Chinese aviation fields 150 miles away from Shanghai on the pretext that they were potentially dangerous to her forces.

At the time of writing (March 24, 1932), Japan has not withdrawn her troops either from Manchuria or Shanghai, in spite of the fact that she claims Manchuria is "self-governed" and that Chinese troops have withdrawn beyond twelve and one-half miles from Shanghai.

Japan Has Broken Three International Treaties

In the opening statement before the League of Nations Assembly on March 3, 1932, the chief Delegate of China, Dr. W. W. Yen, stated:

1. The defiance of the Council by Japan is plain. That the Resolutions of September 30th, and December 10th joined in by the Japanese Government have been absolutely nullified by Japan's military forces appears with axiomatic certainty.

2. Nor is there any room for doubt that the Covenant has been violated. If the forcible seizure of 200,000 square miles of territory and the despatch of any army of 100,000 men to Shanghai do not constitute external aggression, where are the limits to action which can be called non-aggressive under the Covenant? Why did the Twelve Members of the Council in their appeal to Japan bring to her particular attention Article X, if they did not consider that it applies? Article X reads:

The Members of the League undertake to respect and preserve as against external aggression the territorial integrity and existing political independence of all Members of the League. In case of any threat or danger of such aggression the Council shall advise upon the means by which this obligation shall be fulfilled.

Does the undertaking to submit all disputes to arbitration or judicial settlement, as provided in the Covenant have any meaning? Paragraph 1 of Article XII reads:

> The Members of the League agree that, if there should arise between them any dispute likely to lead to a rupture, they will submit the matter either to arbitration or judicial settlement or to inquiry by the Council and they agree in no case to resort to war until three months after the award by the arbitrators or judicial decision, or the report by the Council.

In the very early days of the controversy before the Council, China spread upon the records of the League a written offer to settle all her disputes with Japan by arbitration or judicial settlement in accordance with the terms of the Covenant. When the question was again raised orally by me at the Council meeting of January 29, my Japanese colleague replied as follows:

> The Chinese delegate has stated that Japan has never submitted this conflict to arbitration or to pacific settlement, as is required in accordance with Article XII. That is perfectly true; but it is a well-known fact that Japan is not prepared to accept arbitration with every country irrespectively.

Here is a direct defiance of the Covenant by a formal refusal to arbitrate.

In the appeal to Japan of the Twelve Members of the Council it was said:

> They (the Twelve Members) cannot but regret however, that she (Japan) has not found it possible to make full use of the methods of pacific settlement provided in the Covenant and recall once again the solemn undertakings of the Pact of Paris that the solution of international disputes shall never be sought by other than peaceful means. They cannot but recognize that, from the beginning of the conflict which is taking place in her territory, China has put her case in the hands of the League and agreed to its proposals for a peaceful settlement.

3. That Japan, by refusing to arbitrate, and by resorting to war, has violated the Pact of Paris goes without saying. The Pact says:

Article 1. The High Contracting Parties solemnly declare in the name of their respective peoples that they condemn recourse to war for the solution of international controversies, and renounce it as an instrument of national policy in their relations with one another.

Article 2. The High Contracting Parties agree that the settlement or solution of all disputes or conflicts of whatever origin they may be, which may arise among them, shall never be sought except by pacific means.

4. The violation of the Nine Power Treaty cannot be a matter of indifference to the League which in the Preamble to its Covenant has bound its Members to "a scrupulous respect for all treaty obligations" in their dealings with one another. I venture to remind you of the provisions of that treaty which Japan signed. Article 1 of the Nine Power Treaty provides that the High Contracting Parties other than China agreed:

1. to respect the sovereignty, the independence and the territorial and administrative integrity of China;

2. to provide the fullest and most unembarrassed opportunity to China to develop and maintain for herself an effective and stable government;

3. to use their influence for the purpose of effectually establishing and maintaining the principle of equal opportunity for the commerce and industry of all nations throughout the territory of China;

4. to refrain from taking advantage of conditions in China in order to seek special rights or privileges which would abridge the rights of subjects or citizens of friendly States and from countenancing action inimical to the security of such States.

The American Secretary of State, in his letter to Senator Borah, Chairman of the Foreign Relations Committee of the United States Senate, dated February 25, said:

It must be remembered also that this treaty was one of several treaties and agreements entered into at the Washington Conference by the various Powers concerned, all of which were inter-related and inter-dependent. No one of these treaties can be disregarded without disturbing the general understanding and equilibrium which were intended to be accomplished and effected by the group of agreements arrived at in their entirety. The Washington Conference was essentially a Disarmament Conference aimed to promote the possibility of peace in the world not only through the cessation of competition in naval armament but also by the solution of various other disturbing problems which threatened the peace of the world, particularly in the Far East. These problems were all inter-related. The willingness of the American Government to surrender its then commanding lead in battleship construction and to leave its position at Guam and in the Philippines without further fortification was predicated upon, among other things, the self-denying covenants contained in the Nine Power Treaty which assured the nations of the world not only of equal opportunity for their Eastern trade but also against the military aggrandizement of any other Power at the expense of China. One cannot discuss the possibility of modifying or abrogating those provisions of the Nine Power Treaty without considering at the same time the other promises upon which they were really dependent.

This, in brief, is my country's case before the Assembly. At this very moment of our deliberations, a Chinese territory as large as France and Germany combined is under the iron heel of the invader. Nanking, the capital of my country, has been bombarded for no reason whatsoever. Shanghai, the metropolis of the Far East, has been under the incessant shower of the enemy's bombs and shells. Places where stood busy thoroughfares and magnificent buildings have been demolished by the Japanese artillery and aerial raids and reduced to a heap of ruins wherein lie only the bodies of the heroic dead. Villages and towns have been subjected to the most violent bombings from the air, as witness the latest Japanese aerial expeditions to Soochow and Hangchow upon which tons of explosives were dropped, taking a toll of over seven thousand civilian lives, which cannot but shock the conscience of the civilized world. In truth, the Japanese have been making an undeclared war against China, exploiting all the advantages of war without assuming any of its obligations.

I am coming to the end of my discourse. Where do we stand? We should be closing our eyes to the realities if we did not frankly admit that until now collective mediation has failed. The Council has plead in vain for the cessation of hostilities and withdrawal of the invading forces. It has accepted promises and seen them broken, one after another. It has appealed to Japan's sense of national honor. It has joined the United States in declaring that any situation *de facto* brought about by means contrary to the Covenant, the Pact of Paris and the Nine Power Treaty cannot gain legal recognition. None of these measures had had the slightest effect. Japan's attitude is precisely as intransigeant as it was in the beginning. Her official declaration, delivered only a few days ago in reply to the appeal of the Twelve Members of the Council, embodies a flat refusal to brook any interference on their part. She there announced that she was under no legal promise to do what the Council asked; and that morally she believed she was "naturally and necessarily in a far better position to appreciate the facts than any distant Power can possibly be."

Let us look at the other side of the shield. China places herself unreservedly in the hands of the League; Japan refuses. China offers to adopt any method of peaceful adjustment, including arbitration and judicial settlement, which the League may suggest; Japan refuses. China offers to take full responsibility for the protection of Japanese subjects and interests in Manchuria, with international assistance, after the withdrawal of Japanese troops; Japan refuses to withdraw them. Four Members of the League acting in cooperation with the United States Government proposed a series of measures looking to cessation of hostilities, and the settlement by negotiation of outstanding differences in the spirit of the Pact of Paris and of the Council's resolution of December 10th last; China accepted the proposal *in toto;* Japan rejected them in all their essential features. The neutral Committee of Enquiry set up by your Secretary-General at Shanghai has reported that "a state of war exists and that the offensive is entirely in the hands of the Japanese."

Again, where do we stand:

1. We urge this Extraordinary Assembly which is now seized of the whole dispute between the Republic of China and the

Empire of Japan to explore and exhaust the possibilities of effecting a settlement in conformity with the provisions of our Covenant.

2. China asks you to do everything in your power, first, to bring about the cessation of all hostile action on her territory and the withdrawal of the invading forces; and second, the peaceful settlement of the entire Sino-Japanese controversy within the scope of the Council's Resolutions and the spirit of the Covenant. Naturally, no measure, taken in relation either to Shanghai or to Manchuria, which encroaches upon China's sovereign rights or is contrary to the general principles of International Law or her existing treaty obligations to third parties, can be regarded as a settlement.

3. We ask you to recognize that the Covenant has been broken.

4. We ask you solemnly to declare that for the present terrible state of affairs, which prevails in Manchuria, Shanghai and other parts of China, my country bears no shadow of responsibility. When the Assembly has made this declaration, it will have begun to mobilize those moral forces by which, we still believe, this conflict may be solved and ended.

As a victim of unjustified and unprovoked invasion and even in this hour of battle, I say we cherish no natural animosity against the Japanese people; we should indeed work for our common welfare and for the happiness of all mankind. It is for that reason that we ask for peace with justice which our Covenant prescribes.

Cooperation of the United States

Cooperation of the United States with the League has greatly strengthened the peace machinery. The following two notes are of historical importance because they mark the beginning of concerted action of great powers for peace and for supplementing the League Covenant with the Pact of Paris and the Nine Power Treaty:

On October 9, 1931, the Secretary of State sent to the American consulate at Geneva for communication to the Secretary-General of the League of Nations, a message as follows:

I believe that our co-operation in the future handling of this difficult matter should proceed along the course which has been followed ever since the first outbreak of the trouble fortunately found the Assembly and Council of the League of Nations in session. The Council has deliberated long and earnestly on this matter and the Covenant of the League of Nations provides permanent and already tested machinery for handling such issues as between states members of the League. Both the Chinese and Japanese have presented and argued their cases before the Council, and the world has been informed through published accounts with regard to the proceedings there. The Council has formulated conclusions and outlined a course of action to be followed by the disputants; and as the said disputants have made commitments to the Council, it is most desirable that the League in no way relax its vigilance and in no way fail to assert all the pressure and authority within its competence towards regulating the action of China and Japan in the premises.

On its part the American government, acting independently, through its diplomatic representatives, will endeavor to reinforce what the League does, and will make clear that it has a keen interest in the matter and is not oblivious to the obligations which the disputants have assumed to their fellow signatories in the Pact of Paris as well as in the Nine Power Pact, should a time arise when it would seem advisable to bring forward those obligations. By this course we avoid any danger of embarrassing the League in the course it is now committed.

Again, to the Secretary-General of the League of Nations on March 12, 1932:

The League of Nations at Geneva have united in a common attitude and purpose toward the perilous disturbances in the Far East. The action of the Assembly expresses the purpose for peace which is found both in the Pact of Paris and the Covenant of the League of Nations. In this expression all the nations of the world can speak with the same voice. This action will go far toward developing into terms of international law the principles of order and justice which underlie those treaties and the Government of the United States has been glad to cooperate earnestly in this effort. (League of Nations Document A (Extr.) 49.1932.VII.)

Make the World Safe for Peace

Opinions seem to be divided as to whether the League has suceeded or failed as a peace machinery. Some think that the League has been utterly impotent to check a strong power; others are of the opinion that it has mobilized the moral opinion of the world which is, they say, after all, its most important function.

Whether the League has failed or not, certain questions which have arisen out of the crisis must be answered if peace is to be made secure. For instance, "war" and "self-defense" must be more clearly defined on the basis of facts and not on technicalities and unilateral declarations.

The peace machinery itself does not seem to be equipped for an emergency of major proportions. Although it has been over half a year since Japan occupied Manchuria, the League Commission has not yet arrived at the scene. In forming correct opinions and decisions, it must make sure of its source of information. Some means should be devised for the League to collect data promptly and accurately.

Although there is no doubt that, at least implicitly, the League members unanimously recognize Japan as the aggressor who has violated the Covenant, the League has not been effective in protecting a defenseless nation. While moral opinion is being mobilized, a strong power can inflict irreparable damages upon a comparatively weak country, as has been the case in the present crisis, and create a situation that will take years to disentangle. Of course, the League may refuse to recognize such a situation brought about by actions in violation of Covenant, but the price is too great and it is too much to expect that the victim nation shall sit still patiently waiting for "moral suasion" to restore the *status guo ante,* if it can restore anything at all.

"Moral Suasion" Impotent

The application of economic sanctions under Article XVI is beset with many practical difficulties and involves sacrifices on the part of the members. But the fundamental question remains—what is to be done when a strong power like Japan defies the moral opinion of the world?

Raymond Leslie Buell, Director of Research of the Foreign Policy Association, writes in *The New Republic,* March 9, 1932:

> Others urge that, despite the failure to check Japan by "moral suasion," matters should be allowed to take their course, since Japan will ultimately suffer from its present venture and China ultimately will triumph. Would that this romantic theory that Good always conquers Evil were sound! This theory, however, could be applied to any war in history, and if true, it would make all peace machinery unnecessary. What it overlooks is the tremendous amount of suffering caused by the process of war—suffering which cannot be obliterated by the ultimate triumph of Good. Japan may not be strong enough to conquer and successfully exploit China; but it will probably prove strong enough to throw China into complete anarchy and bring about the utter demoralization of the Orient.

Such a result is bound to be harmful to the Japanese and all other peoples. For this very reason any process leading to such a result should be arrested as soon as possible. The weakness of Secretary Stimson's refusal to recognize the legal validity of any settlement made by Japan in violation of the anti-war pact is that it does nothing to prevent the suffering caused by war. Moreover, it is doubtful whether this 'legal' sanction alone will be any more effective in checkmating Japan than non-recognition has been in forcing Soviet Russia to pay its debts or the 1923 Central American treaty has been in preventing revolution.

Thus the "business as usual" policy strengthens Japanese militarism and does a grave injustice to China. It likewise deals a vital blow to the international peace institutions which have been built up so laboriously since the World War. The failure to stop Japan's aggressions has already increased the sentiment that a nation's security must rest upon armaments; it has bolstered militarism and imperialism in every country. I am satisfied, therefore, that in opposing the principle of economic sanctions, *The New Republic* and its followers are unwittingly joining hands with the Tories of Great Britain, the Nationalists of France and the Hearst press in undermining the principle of international solidarity and in reviving a jungle world. Pascal was right when he said: 'Justice without might is unavailing, for the wicked are ever with us. Might without justice stands condemned. We must therefore mete justice with might and to that end we must ensure that what is just is mighty and that what is mighty is just.'

President A. Lawrence Lowell of Harvard University in a radio address broadcast on February 17, 1932, said: "The events in Manchuria, and still more at Shanghai, have shown that mere protests by other governments, and the public opinion of neutrals, will not alone restrain the use of armed force to attend a nation's end."

CHAPTER XX

JAPAN'S CHALLENGE

Verdict of Mankind

"THE ASSEMBLY OF THE LEAGUE OF NATIONS which is now meeting on the appeal of China is in theory a stupendous affair!" wrote Walter Lippmann from Geneva on March 7, 1932. "It is the nearest thing to a parliament of mankind ever assembled on earth." He commented further:

There are only three important nations not formally represented —the Argentine, Russia and the United States. In fact, both Russia and the United States are actually present and the United States, though it does not attend the public sessions, is in the thick of innermost proceedings. In so far as the governments can express the conscience and will of humanity, this Assembly of Governments has all the necessary credentials entitling it to deliver a great collective judgment upon the Oriental War.

The unanimity of opinion of all 46 countries represented is without precedent. All and everyone of the representatives has definitely expressed the opinion that Japan has waged war and that Japan cannot justify her actions upon grounds of self-defense.

On March 4, 1932, the "Parliament of Mankind" rendered its verdict. The scene of how this momentous decision was reached is worth recording. Clarence K. Streit reported to the New York *Times,* as follows:

Geneva, March 4.—The League of Nations Assembly, with Japan's agreement, voted unanimously by roll-call tonight a resolution calling for the unconditional withdrawal of Japanese forces from the Shanghai area.

This clean-cut victory on what Japan had for four hours bitterly fought for as an "essential" point was dramatically won for the League by the courage of three men, and of these three men alone. Their names, in the order in which they went to battle, are Paul Hymans, Foreign Minister of Belgium and president of the Assembly; Giuseppe Motta, President of Switzerland, and Edouard Benes, Foreign Minister of Czechoslovakia.

Things came to a showdown. When they did these leaders of three small European countries—two of them landlocked and another that has abolished its navy—won more from Japanese diplomacy than all the great naval powers have won from it in five months. They were vigorously applauded by the others.

To M. Hymans goes the credit of calling a spade a spade by declaring the resolution's verbiage really meant an unconditional Japanese withdrawal and of forcing a showdown by appealing to the fifty member States to support him in this when Japan demanded certain conditions as essential.

Silence Answers Plea at First

To M. Motta belongs the credit of breaking the deathly silence that for a long moment was the Assembly's answer to M. Hymans's imploring appeal. That silence was such that when M. Motta rose a storm of applause rose spontaneously from most of the diplomats, although they are trained never to applaud. Quivering with emotion, M. Motta spoke briefly and strongly. He not only re-inforced M. Hymans, but he raised the League's standard still higher. He asked Naotake Sato, the Japanese delegate, to accept the resolution as it stood, warning him that the Assembly now had the power to adopt it without Japan's consent. When M. Motta sat down the diplomats applauded even more than before. And men shook hands with their nearest Swiss friends and congratulated them on having such a President.

To M. Benes belongs the credit of immediately rising and unequivocally backing M. Motta.

Assembly Again Silent

How courageous and how strong these two had been was then driven home, for of all these who had applauded them not one rose to follow suit. That deathly silence settled down again. But in it Mr. Sato apparently decided that when the world heard of this the world would stand with Messrs. Hymans, Motta and Benes, and not sit speechless, like its diplomats there in the hall. Mr. Sato broke the second silence to renounce Japan's amendment and to tell Mr. Motta he would accept, although ten minutes earlier he had said Japan could not possibly accept the resolution as it stood.

As the New York *Times* reported on March 5, 1932:

Fifteen small powers, scattered through four continents, spoke. Their authority and strength lay in the fact that neither party could reasonably suspect a single one of them of being influenced in its judgments by any of the direct material interests all the great powers have in this dispute.

"Spontaneously and absolutely," as Giuseppe Motta of Switzerland put it, "all the fifteen spokesmen, each reading a prepared State paper, agreed on every basic issue. It was impressive."

The following abstracts are from the speeches by some of the small powers. (From the Verbatim Report of the Extraordinary Session of the Assembly of the League of Nations):

I do not propose at this point to expatiate on certain natural ideas concerning legitimate defence; legitimate defence has been used as a cloak, but I do not think one can take cover behind that argument until all the pacific and protective procedures provided for in the Covenant have been exhausted. (By M. Motta of Switzerland.)

It is the internal weakness of certain countries and the strength of others which has made the Covenant more than ever necessary. The League of Nations, the organ of the international community, owes it to itself to protect internationally the weak against the power of the strong, and the strong against the anarchy of the weak. If therefore cases of conflict occur owing to a lack of internel organisation in certain countries it is, we think, to Geneva that such cases should be brought; but we could not support any view to the effect that in such a case any individual State has a right to take exceptional and individual action. (By M. Zulueta of Spain.)

On the contrary, in virtue of the Covenant, whilst the country has a right to proceed to legitimate defence, it has not the right to seek justice by its own means. It might indeed do it with the authorisation of the League; but in the absence of any such authorisation, and in the case of action of such a great scope and such political importance undertaken by one of the parties to the dispute on the territory of the other, I cannot but recall the provisions of Article 10— one of the fundamental Articles of the Covenant—which seem to me to have been infringed. (By M. Benes of Czechoslovakia.)

Powerful Japanese forces, equipped with all the modern weapons of war, have been transported into Chinese territory. These armies have been actively and destructively used against Chinese forces and have taken possession of a considerable portion of Chinese territory. It appears to us equally clear that Japan has not sought to use the pacific means at its disposal under the Covenant of the League, to which it is signatory. Nor, in the absence of any further explanation by Japan, does it appear to us that in this dispute she has remembered her declarations under the Pact of Paris. Equally it seems to my delegation an undisputed fact that China has placed its case in the hands of the League and has been prepared at every stage of the enquiry by the Council of the League to act on its advice and instructions; as emphatically has Japan refused to show the same confidence in the fairmindedness of a body of which it has been for many years so active and important a Member.

As far as these facts are concerned, it is to be stated unhesitatingly, in our opinion, that a *prima facie* case has been made out that Japan has acted in contradiction of what we believe to be the obligations to which, equally with all of us, she is bound. (By Mr. C. T. te Water of South Africa, British Empire.)

On March 11th, the Assembly placed itself on record in a resolution "not to recognize any situation, treaty or agreement which may be brought about by means contrary to the

Covenant of the League of Nations or the Pact of Paris."
In this the forty-six nations have taken the same stand as
that of the United States.

Unacceptable to Japan

Developments since then have made it clear that Japan
does not intend to accept the verdict of mankind to arbitrate
her differences with China. In his recent speech before the
Japanese Diet, Foreign Minister Yoshizawa asserted, on
March 21st, that the "Assembly passed a resolution on
March 11th which was in more than one respect unaccept-
able to our government."

More than that. She has occupied and is now ruling or
attempting to rule a large section of China. She has destroyed a section of Shanghai and is now occupying a zone
of twelve and a half miles beyond Shanghai.

Japan is challenging the fundamental principles of
justice and peace upon which the New International Order
stands. Have not the Chinese people the right to freely
work out their own political destiny? Should Japan be
permitted to be the accuser, judge, jury and executioner in
disputes to which she is an interested party? The principle
of self-determination that the Thirteen Colonies fought for
and the peace machinery that has been built up since the
Great War have been demolished by the Japanese army and
navy.

Japan's challenge is ably stated by Walter Lippmann in
an editorial published by the New York *Herald Tribune* on
Feb. 23, 1932:

The principle of the note of Jan. 7th, is that illegal force can no longer establish legal rights. In the past, the use of force has been legal and its results have been recognized. In the post-war world military force used as an instrument of national policy is illegal and its results are therefore invalid. That is where we stand today, we and all the powers except Japan. The event will show whether we can make good our declaration, whether in the long run law can be vindicated against force.

APPENDICES

APPENDICES

Appendix I

STATEMENT OF THE CHINESE GOVERNMENT
February 12, 1932.

With full realization of its responsibility to the civilized world and willingness to submit the accuracy of those statements to impartial international enquiry and adjudication, the Chinese National Government presents the following summary of the Sino-Japanese conflict from its inception:

At no time since the Russo-Japanese War has the Chinese Government doubted the purpose of Japan to seize Manchuria whenever on opportune occasion arose. At the conclusion of the Russo-Japanese War, which was fought chiefly on China's soil against China's protests, Japan put strong pressure on China to implement Japan's gains from Russia and to grant Japan additional special privileges, impairing China's sovereignty and contravening the "open-door" policy in Manchuria. China resisted those demands to the utmost of her ability.

When the World War arose, Japan took advantage of the preoccupation of the Powers and China's military weakness to present the twenty-one demands which, if conceded, would have destroyed China's sovereignty, not only in Manchuria, but in other parts of China as well. Under Japan's ultimatum, China was forced to concede some of those demands, which she did under protest and so notified all the friendly Powers.

At the Paris Conference, at the Washington Conference, and before the League of Nations, China reiterated her protests against those exactions of Japan and repudiated them all at suitable occasions. At the Washington Conference, China refused to conduct separate negotiations with Japan and insisted that Sino-Japanese questions must be discussed in purview of the whole Conference.

By signing the Nine Power Treaty of Washington, China's territorial integrity and administrative autonomy were guaranteed by all the Powers and it was definitely stated that Manchuria is an integral part of China's territory. That Treaty also provided for appeal to the signatory Powers in the event of disagreement about the interpretation of the Treaty and the infracion of its terms.

Subsequent to signing the Nine Power Treaty, the Chinese Government has invariably in its relations with Japan and other Powers insisted upon observing the terms and the principles of that Treaty, but, owing to Japan's continuously trying to step outside the Treaty and to insist upon having special rights in China, especially in Manchuria, the Chinese Government has been unable to avoid disputes and frictions with Japan which, when serious, China tried to refer to the League of Nations and the Court of International Justice. China gladly became party to the Kellogg-Briand Pact renouncing force as a means to settle international disputes and obtain political objectives and has associated herself with all similar plans to secure peace. On several occasions China sought without success to invoke provisions of the League of Nations Covenant that obsolete and unsatisfactory treaties might be revised.

This, broadly, was the situation last September when, without provocation, Japanese troops attacked Chinese troops at Mukden and usurped control there. A careful analysis shows without doubt that Japan's military coup was premeditated and carefully planned. Dispositions were commenced days before September 18th.

It is scarcely necessary to review events in Manchuria since then. Using various pretexts, the Japanese army has overturned Chinese authority in Manchuria and taken control almost of the whole of these provinces, while China appealed in vain to the League of Nations and the peace pacts.

At times since the Mukden attack, Japan tried to draw the Chinese Government into separate negotiations, but China, following precedents set at Paris, Washington and Geneva, has refused to negotiate without the presence or participation of neutral Powers, knowing full well that she cannot singly resist Japan's pressure backed by unbridled military force which aims at the annexation of Manchuria.

Those tactics failing to frighten the Chinese Government, Japan decided to carry military action into the heart of China, showing her contempt for and indifference to world opinion, with the purpose of convincing the Chinese that it was hopeless to appeal for outside help. During the four months of continuous Japanese military aggression, the indignation of the Chinese people was aroused to the highest pitch, while the Chinese Government, already harassed by natural calamities, was faced with the task of dealing with invasion from without and restraining popular feeling within.

Having sent naval forces to Shanghai with the stated purpose of protecting Japanese residents and property there, the Japanese Government presented through the Japanese Consul-General certain demands to the Chinese local authorities at Shanghai, requiring complete acquiescence by six o'clock P.M. on January 28th. At two o'clock that afternoon, the Chinese replied fully accepting Japan's demand and were assured by the Japanese Consul-General that the reply was satisfactory. Nevertheless, at midnight that night, Japanese naval forces advanced into Chinese territory and attacked the Chinese police and garrison troops. The Chinese Government has no doubt that disinterested foreigners on the scene have more or less correctly informed the world of events at Shanghai since January 28th, but the Chinese Government wishes to emphasise the following points:

The Japanese naval and military forces have used the International Settlement at Shanghai both as a base for their attacks on the Chinese police and troops and as a sanctuary where they can retire when repulsed and for recuperation and re-supply.

The Chinese troops, in defending China's soil from ruthless invaders, have been unable to reply effectively to the Japanese attacks without endangering the lives and property of thousands of friendly neutral foreigners residing in the International Settlement and surrounding suburbs and have been unable to pursue their Japanese attackers without risking a conflict with friendly neutral foreign police and troops protecting the Settlement.

The Japanese naval and military forces have used the river-front docks within the International Settlement to land troops, artillery and supplies. Japanese warships anchored in the Whangpoo River alongside the International Settlement fire over the Settlement at Chinese forces resisting Japanese attacks in Chinese territory outside the Settlement, and Chinese artillery cannot reply effectively without gravely endangering scores of neutral vessels in port. The

Japanese flagship with the Japanese admiral and staff directing attacks lies alongside the wharf near the centre of the Settlement.

Japanese airplanes bombed all parts of Chinese districts of Shanghai, also parts of the International Settlement and then withdrew over the midsection of the International Settlement.

Japanese military forces and civilian un-uniformed elements have killed and injured presently large number of Chinese peaceable unarmed men, women, children, estimated between one and two thousand, and imprisoned, maltreated many others and executed many without trial.

Japanese bombings and fires started by bombs already have destroyed property roughly estimated at hundreds of millions of dollars.

The Japanese Government excuses these atrocities by allleging the military peril due to proximity of Chinese troops. The Chinese Government solemnly declares that such excuse is a transparent pretext, as it is impossible to send Japanese troops anywhere in China without being surrounded by Chinese population and near Chinese troops occupying their regular stations. Japanese military forces have pushed forward into China's territory, always making the excuse that nearby Chinese troops constitute a menace. It is evident that such reasoning provides excuse for the complete conquest of China by Japan.

When the United States of America and Great Britain, supported by France, Germany and Italy, recently presented to Japan and China a note in five points designed to end hostilities and to bring about the liquidation of this situation worse than war, the Chinese Government without hesitation accepted the proposals of the Powers in full.

In flatly turning down, first, the proposals of the International Shanghai Defence Committee, then the Powers' five proposals and more recently still the British Admiral Kelly's scheme, Japan is thus closing every avenue to peace, leaving China no alternative but to continue to adopt appropriate measures for self-defence to the best of her ability.

The Chinese Government asks the world to contrast known facts of Japan's acts in China during recent months with the Japanese Government's latest statement that "it is the immutable policy of the Japanese Government to ensure tranquillity in the Far East." Also to contrast Japan's statement that "her troops in China are only to discharge an international duty" with the efforts of the League of Nations and Washington Treaty Powers to induce Japan to withdraw her troops from China and to cease warfare. Also contrast Japan's frequent declarations that she has no territorial ambitions vis-a-vis China with her refusal to submit the Manchurian and other Sino-Japanese questions before a conference of Treaty Powers. Also contrast Japan's acts at Shanghai causing immense destruction of the property of all nationals and loss of lives with her statement that she acted in Shanghai in co-operation with the other foreign defence forces and foreign municipal authorities and with the latest statement of the Shanghai foreign Municipal Council that "Japanese Government and not the Municipal Council is solely responsible for acts of the Japanese armed forces in Shanghai."

The Chinese Government positively denies that the Chinese violated the temporary truce arranged on January 29th. Because of the suddenness of the armistice, it was not possible to get orders to all outposts resulting, during the night, in desultory firing between the outposts on both sides. The Japanese command resumed attacks at daybreak of January 30th.

Since Japan's astounding action in Mukden last September, it has been the unswerving policy of the Chinese Government to avoid, by all means at its command, a state of war and to that end it has endured intense humiliation, risked its own existence in face of popular feeling, in the hope that the worldwide pacific measures might check Japan's reckless course. Despite the failure so far of the pacific agencies, the Chinese Government adheres to its faith in world justice, but it cannot passively submit to Japan's invasion of China's territory and slaughter of Chinese people. It therefore solemnly declares to the world that China will continue to resist in self-defence Japan's attacks at all points and with all the forces at its command.

The Chinese Government further declares that it is China's desire to settle issues in connection with the present crisis in purview of interested Powers and in accordance with principles guaranteeing world peace and the sovereignty, independence, and territorial and administrative integrity of China.

STATEMENT OF THE CHINESE GOVERNMENT CON-
CERNING THE SO-CALLED INDEPENDENCE
MOVEMENT IN MANCHURIA

February 22, 1932.

The Three Eastern Provinces, also known as Manchuria, are
always an integral part of China and any usurpation or interference
with the administration therein constitutes a direct impairment of
China's territorial and administrative integrity. Article I of the Or-
ganic Law of the National Government of October 4, 1928, which
was proclaimed in Manchuria as well as the other provinces of the
Republic provides that the National Government will exercise all
the governing powers of the Chinese Republic. The Provisional
Constitution of June 1, 1931, expressly provides that the territory of
the Chinese Republic consists of the various provinces, Mongolia, and
Tibet, and that the Chinese Republic will be a unified Republic forever.

The territorial, political and administrative integrity of the Chinese Republic, besides being an attribute of a sovereign state according
to the international law is guaranteed by Article X of the League
Covenant and Article I of the Nine Power Treaty. Such guarantee
has been implemented by Japan when she adhered to the League
Council Resolution of the 30th of last September—

"The Council

2. Recognizes the importance of the Japanese Government's
statement that it has no territorial designs in Manchuria;

"5. Being convinced that both Governments are anxious to
avoid taking any action which might disturb the peace and good
understanding between the two nations, notes that the Chinese
and Japanese representatives have given assurances that their respective Governments will take all necessary steps to prevent any
extension of the scope of the incident or any aggravation of the
situation."

In the resolution of the 24th of last October the Council emphasized the importance of these assurances saying that it—

"(3) Recalls the Japanese statement that Japan has no territorial designs in Manchuria, and notes that this statement is in accordance with the terms of the Covenant of the League of Nations, and of the Nine Power Treaty, the signatories of which are pledged 'to respect the sovereignty, the independence, and the territorial and administrative integrity of China.'"

The Council further notes in the Resolution of the 10th of last December—

"(2) Considering that events have assumed an even more serious aspect since the Council meeting of October 24th;
(The Council) "Notes that the two parties undertake to adopt all measures necessary to avoid any further aggravation of the situation and to refrain from any initiative which may lead to further fighting and loss of life."

This Resolution was also accepted by Japan. The Chinese Delegate who endorsed it declared:

"China would regard any attempt by Japan to bring about complications of a political character affecting China's territorial or administrative integrity (such as promoting so-called independence movements, or utilizing disorderly elements for such purposes) as an obvious violation of the undertaking to avoid any further aggravation of the situation."

Now in defiance of all law and solemn obligations the Japanese authorities who are in unlawful occupation of the Three Eastern Provinces are endeavoring to set up in these Provinces a so-called independent government and are trying to compel the Chinese citizens to participate in the puppet organization. The National Government has repeatedly and emphatically protested against the illegal actions of the Japanese Government and hereby again declares that it will not recognize the secession or independence of the Three Eastern Provinces or any part thereof or any administration which may be organized therein without its authority and consent.

TEXT OF SECRETARY STIMSON'S NOTE OF JANUARY 7, 1932

Following is the text of the note that Secretary Stimson sent on January 7, 1932, to the governments of China and Japan, copies of which were also handed by the Secretary of State to the diplomatic representatives of Belgium, Great Britain, France, Italy, The Netherlands and Portugal:

With the recent military operations about Chinchow, the last remaining administrative authority of the government of the Chinese Republic in South Manchuria, as it existed prior to Sept. 18, 1931, has been destroyed. The American Government continues confident that the work of the neutral commission recently authorized by the Council of the League of Nations will facilitate an ultimate solution of the difficulties now existing between China and Japan.

But in view of the present situation and of its own rights and obligations therein, the American Government deems it to be its duty to notify both the Imperial Japanese Government and the government of the Chinese Republic:

That it cannot admit the legality of any situation de facto, nor does it intend to recognize any treaty or agreement entered into between those governments, or grants thereof, which may impair the treaty rights of the United States or its citizens in China, including those which relate to the sovereignty, the independence or the territorial and administrative integrity of the Republic of China, or to the international policy relative to China, commonly known as the open door policy;

And that it does not intend to recognize any situation, treaty or agreement which may be brought about by means contrary to the covenants and obligations of the Pact of Paris of Aug. 27, 1928, to which treaty both China and Japan, as well as the United States, are parties.

TEXT OF STIMSON'S LETTER TO SENATOR BORAH, FEB. 24, 1932

My Dear Senator Borah:

You have asked my opinion whether, as has been sometimes recently suggested, present conditions in China have in any way indicated that the so-called Nine Power Treaty has become inapplicable or ineffective or right in need of modification, and, if so, what I considered should be the policy of this government.

This treaty, as you, of course, know, forms the legal basis upon which now rests the "open door" policy toward China. That policy, enunciated by John Hay in 1899, brought to an end the struggle among various powers for so-called spheres of interest in China which was threatening the dismemberment of that empire.

To accomplish this Mr. Hay invoked two principles:

(1) Equality of commercial opportunity among all nations in dealing with China, and

(2) As necessary to that equality the preservation of China's territorial and administrative integrity.

These principles were not new in the foreign policy of America. They had been the principles upon which it rested in its dealings with other nations for many years. In the case of China they were invoked to save a situation which not only threatened the future development and sovereignty of that great Asiatic people, but also threatened to create dangerous and constantly increasing rivalries between the other nations of the world.

War had already taken place between Japan and China. At the close of that war three other nations intervened to prevent Japan from obtaining some of the results of that war claimed by her. Other nations sought and had obtained spheres of interest.

Hay's Statement of Policy

Partly as a result of these actions a serious uprising had broken out in China which endangered the legations of all of the powers at Peking. While the attack on those legations was in progress Mr.

Hay made an announcement in respect to this policy as the principle upon which the powers should act in the settlement of the rebellion. He said:

"The policy of the Government of the United States is to seek a solution which may bring about permanent safety and peace to China, preserve Chinese territorial and administrative entity, protect all rights guaranteed to friendly powers by treaty and international law, and safeguard for the world the principle of equal and impartial trade with all parts of the Chinese Empire."

He was successful in obtaining the assent of the other powers to the policy thus announced.

In taking these steps Mr. Hay acted with the cordial support of the British Government. In responding to Mr. Hay's announcement, above set forth, Lord Salisbury, the British Prime Minister, expressed himself "most emphatically as concurring in the policy of the United States."

For twenty years thereafter the open door policy rested upon the informal commitments thus made by the various powers. But in the Winter of 1921 to 1922, at a conference participated in by all of the principal powers which had interests in the Pacific, the policy was crystallized into the so-called Nine Power Treaty, which gave definition and precision to the principles upon which the policy rested. In the first article of that treaty, the contracting powers, other than China agreed

1. To respect the sovereignty, the independence and the territorial and administrative integrity of China.

2. To provide the fullest and most unembarrassed opportunity to China to develop and maintain for herself an effective and stable government.

3. To use their influence for the purpose of effectually establishing and maintaining the principle of equal opportunity for the commerce and industry of all nations throughout the territory of China.

4. To refrain from taking advantage of conditions in China in order to seek special rights or privileges which would abridge the rights of subjects or citizens of friendly States, and from countenancing action inimical to the security of such States.

"A Covenant of Self-Denial"

This treaty thus represents a carefully developed and matured international policy intended, on the one hand, to assure to all of the contracting parties their rights and interests in and with regard to China, and on the other hand, to assure to the people of China the fullest opportunity to develop without molestation their sovereignty and independence according to the modern and enlightened standards believed to maintain among the peoples of this earth.

At the time this treaty was signed, it was known that China was engaged in an attempt to develop the free institutions of a self-governing republic after her recent revolution from an autocratic form of government; that she would require many years of both economic and political effort to that end, and that her progress would necessarily be slow.

The treaty was thus a covenant of self-denial among the signatory powers in deliberate renunciation of any policy of aggression which might tend to interfere with that development. It was believed—and the whole history of that development of the "open door" policy reveals that faith—that only by such a process, under the protection of such an agreement, could the fullest interests not only of China but of all nations which have intercourse with her best be served.

In its report to the President announcing this treaty the American delegation, headed by the then Secretary of State, Mr. Charles E. Hughes, said:

"It is believed that through this treaty the 'open door' in China has at last been made a fact."

British and Japanese Positions

During the course of the discussions which resulted in the treaty the chairman of the British delegation, Lord Balfour, had stated that:

"The Brtitish Empire delegation understood that there was no representative of any power around the table who thought that the old practice of 'spheres of interest' was either advocated by any government or would be tolerable to this conference. So far as the British Government were concerned, they had, in the most formal manner, publicly announced that they regarded this practice as utterly inappropriate to the existing situation."

At the same time, the representative of Japan, Baron Shidehara, announced the position of his government as follows:

"No one denies to China her sacred right to govern herself. No one stands in the way of China to work out her own great national destiny."

The treaty was originally executed by the United States, Belgium, the British Empire, China, France, Italy, Japan, The Netherlands and Portugal. Subsequently it was also executed by Norway, Bolivia, Sweden, Denmark and Mexico. Germany has signed it, but her Parliament has not yet ratified it.

It must be remembered also that this treaty was one of the several treaties and agreements entered into at the Washington Conference by the various powers concerned, all of which were interrelated and interdependent.

No one of these treaties can be disregarded without disturbing the general understanding and equilibrium which were intended to be accomplished and effected by the group of agreements arrived at in their entirety.

The Washington Conference was essentially a disarmament conference, aimed to promote the possibility of peace in the world, not only through the cessation of competition in naval armament, but also by the solution of various other disturbing problems which threatened the peace of the world, particularly in the Far East. These problems were all interrelated.

Treaties Are Linked Together

The willingness of the American Government to surrender its then commanding lead in battleship construction and to leave its positions at Guam and in the Philippines without further fortifications was predicated upon, among other things, the self-denying covenants contained in the Nine Power Treaty, which assured the nations of the world not only of equal opportunity for their Eastern trade, but also against the military aggrandizement of any other power at the expense of China.

One cannot discuss the possibility of modifying or abrogating those provisions of the Nine Power Treaty without considering at the same time the other promises upon which they were really dependent.

Six years later the policy of self-denial against aggression by a stronger against a weaker power, upon which the Nine Power Treaty had been based, received a powerful reinforcement by the execution by substantially all the nations of the world of the Pact of Paris, the so-called Kellogg-Briand pact.

These two treaties represent independent but harmonious steps taken for the purpose of aligning the conscience and public opinion of the world in favor of a system of orderly development by the law of nations, including the settlement of all controversies by methods of justice and peace instead of by arbitrary force.

The program for the protection of China from outside aggression is an essential part of any such development. The signatories and adherents of the Nine Power Treaty felt that the orderly and peaceful development of the 400,000,000 of people inhabiting China was necessary to the peaceful welfare of the entire world, and that no program for the welfare of the world as a whole could afford to neglect the welfare and protection of China.

No Need of Modification Shown

The recent events which have taken place in China, especially the hostilities, which, having been begun in Manchuria, have latterly been extended to Shanghai, far from indicating the advisability of any modification of the treaties we have been discussing, have tended to bring home the vital importance of the faithful observance of the covenants therein to all of the nations interested in the Far East.

It is not necessary in that connection to inquire into the causes of the controversy or attempt to apportion the blame between the two nations which are unhappily involved; for, regardless of cause or responsibility, it is clear beyond peradventure that a situation has developed which cannot, under any circumstances, be reconciled with the obligations of the covenants of these two treaties, and that if the treaties had been faithfully observed such a situation could not have arisen.

The signatories of the Nine Power Treaty and of the Kellogg-Briand pact who are not parties to that conflict are not likely to see any reason for modifying the terms of those treaties. To them the real value of the faithful performance of the treaties has been brought sharply home by the perils and losses to which their nations have been subjected in Shanghai.

This is the view of this government:

We see no reason for abandoning, the enlightened principles which are embodied in these treaties.

We believe that this situation would have been avoided had these covenants been faithfully observed. And no evidence has come to us to indicate that a due compliance with them would have interfered with the adequate protection of the legitimate rights in China of the signatories of those treaties and their nations.

On Jan. 7 last, upon the instruction of the President, this government formally notified Japan and China that it would not recognize any situation, treaty or agreement entered into by those governments in violation of the covenants of these treaties, which affected the rights of our government or its citizens in China.

Suggests Action by Other Powers

If a similar decision should be reached and a similar position taken by the other governments of the world, a caveat will be placed upon such action which, we believe, will effectively bar the legality hereafter of any title or right sought to be obtained by pressure or treaty violation, and which, as has been shown by history in the past, will eventually lead to the restoration to China of rights and titles of which she may have been deprived.

In the past our government, as one of the leading powers on the Pacific Ocean, has rested its policy upon an abiding faith in the future of the people of China and upon the ultimate success in dealing with them of the principles of fair play, patience and mutual goodwill. We appreciate the immensity of the task which lies before her statesmen in the development of her country and its government.

The delays in her progress, the instability of her attempts to secure a responsible government, were foreseen by Messrs. Hay and Hughes and their contemporaries and were the very obstacles which the policy of the open door was designed to meet.

We concur with those statesmen, representing all the nations in the Washington conference who decided that China was entitled to the time necessary to accomplish her development. We are prepared to make that our policy for the future.

Very sincerely yours,

HENRY L. STIMSON

As published in the New York *Times*, February 25, 1932.

APPENDIX V

ARTICLES OF THE COVENANT OF THE LEAGUE OF NATIONS THAT ARE RELEVANT TO THE PRESENT DISPUTE

The High Contracting Parties,

In order to promote international cooperation and to achieve international peace and security

by the acceptance of obligations not to resort to war,

by the prescription of open, just and honorable relations between nations,

by the firm establishment of the understandings of international law as the actual rule of conduct among Governments, and

by the maintenance of justice and a scrupulous respect for all treaty obligations in the dealings of organized peoples with one another,

Agree to this Covenant of the League of Nations.

ARTICLE X

Guarantee Against Aggression

The Members of the League undertake to respect and preserve as against external aggression the territorial integrity and existing political independence of all members of the League. In case of any such aggression or in case of any threat or danger of such aggression, the Council shall advise upon the means by which this obligation shall be fulfilled.

ARTICLE XI

Action in Case of War or Threat of War

1. Any war or threat of war, whether immediately affecting any of the Members of the League or not, is hereby declared a matter of concern to the whole League, and the League shall take any action that may be deemed wise and effectual to safeguard the peace of nations. In case any such emergency should arise, the Secretary-General shall, on the request of any Member of the League, forthwith summon a meeting of the Council.

2. It is also declared to be the friendly right of each Member of the League to bring to the attention of the Assembly or of the Council any circumstance whatever affecting international relations which threatens to disturb international peace or the good understanding between nations upon which peace depends.

ARTICLE XII

Disputes to be Submitted for Settlement

1. The Members of the League agree that, if there should arise between them any dispute to lead to a rupture they will submit the matter either to arbitration or judicial settlement or to inquiry by the Council and they agree in no case to resort to war until three months after the award by arbitrators or the judicial decision, or the report by the Council.

2. In any case under this Article, the award of the arbitrators or the judicial decision shall be made within a reasonable time, and the report of the Council shall be made within six months after the submission of the dispute.

ARTICLE XIII

Arbitration or Judicial Settlement

1. The Members of the League agree that, whenever any dispute shall arise between them which they recognize to be suitable for submission to arbitration or judicial settlement, and which can not be satisfactorily settled by diplomacy, they will submit the whole subject-matter to arbitration or judicial settlement.

2. Disputes as to the interpretation of a treaty, as to any question of international law, as to the existence of any fact which, if established, would constitute a breach of any international obligation, or as to the extent and nature of the reparation to be made for any such breach, are declared to be among those which are generally suitable for submission to arbitration or judicial settlement.

3. For the consideration of any such dispute, the court to which the case is referred shall be the Permanent Court of International Justice, established in accordance with Article XIV, or any tribunal agreed on by the parties to the dispute or stipulated in any convention existing between them.

4. The Members of the League agree that they will carry out in full good faith any award or decision that may be rendered, and that they will not resort to war against a Member of the League which complies therewith. In the event of any failure to carry out such an award or decision, the Council shall propose what steps should be taken to give effect thereto.

Article XIV

Permanent Court of International Justice

The Council shall formulate and submit to the Members of the League for adoption plans for the establishment of a Permanent Court of International Justice. The Court shall be competent to hear and determine any dispute of an international character which the parties thereto submit to it. The Court may also give an advisory opinion upon any dispute or question referred to it by the Council or by the Assembly.

Article XV

Disputes Not Submitted to Arbitration or Judicial Settlement

1. If there should arise between Members of the League any dispute likely to lead to a rupture, which is not submitted to arbitration or judicial settlement in accordance with Article XIII, the Members of the League agree that they will submit the matter to the Council. Any party to the dispute may effect such submission by giving notice of the existence of the dispute to the Secretary-General, who will

make all necessary arrangements for a full investigation and consideration thereof.

2. For this purpose the parties to the dispute will communicate to the Secretary-General, as promptly as possible, statements of their case, with all the relevant facts and papers, and the Council may forthwith direct the publication thereof.

3. The Council shall endeavor to effect a settlement of the dispute and, if such efforts are successful, a statement shall be made public giving such facts and explanations regarding the dispute and the terms of settlement thereof as the Council may deem appropriate.

4. If the dispute is not thus settled, the Council either unanimously or by a majority vote, shall make and publish a report containing a statement of the facts of the dispute and the recommendations which are deemed just and proper in regard thereto.

5. Any Member of the League represented on the Council may make public a statement of the facts of the dispute and of its conclusions regarding the same.

6. If a report by the Council is unanimously agreed to by the Members thereof other than the Representatives of one or more of the parties to the dispute, the Members of the League agree that they will not go to war with any party to the dispute which complies with the recommendations of the report.

7. If the Council fails to reach a report which is unanimously agreed to by the members thereof, other than the Representatives of one or more of the parties to the dispute, the Members of the League reserve to themselves the right to take such action as they shall consider necessary for the maintenance of right and justice.

8. If the dispute between the parties is claimed by one of them, and is found by the Council, to arise out of a matter which by international law is solely within the domestic jurisdiction of that party, the Council shall so report, and shall make no recommendations as to its settlement.

9. The Council may in any case under this article refer the dispute to the Assembly. The dispute shall be so referred at the request of either party to the dispute, provided that such request be made within 14 days after the submission of the dispute to the Council.

10. In any case referred to the Assembly, all the provisions of this Article and of Article XII relating to the action and powers of

the Council shall apply to the action and powers of the Assembly, provided that a report made by the Assembly, if concurred in by the Representatives of a majority of the other Members of the League, exclusive in each case of the Representatives of the parties to the dispute shall have the same force as a report by the Council concurred in by all the members thereof other than the Representatives of one or more of the parties to the dispute.

ARTICLE XVI
Sanctions of Pacific Settlement

1. Should any Member of the League resort to war in disregard of its covenants under Articles XII, XIII or XV, it shall *ipso facto* be deemed to have committed an act of war against all other Members of the League, which hereby undertake immediately to subject it to the severance of all trade or financial relations, the prohibition of all intercourse between their nationals and the nationals of the covenant-breaking State, and the prevention of all financial, commercial or personal intercourse between the nationals of the covenant-breaking State and the nationals of any other State, whether a Member of the League or not.

2. It shall be the duty of the Council in such case to recommend to the several Governments concerned what effective military, naval or air force the Members of the League shall severally contribute to the armed forces to be used to protect the covenants of the League.

3. The Members of the League agree, further, that they will mutually support one another in the financial and economic measures which are taken under this Article, in order to minimize the loss and inconvenience resulting from the above measures, and that they will mutually support one another in resisting any special measures aimed at one of their number by the covenant-breaking State, and that they will take the necessary steps to afford passage through their territory to the forces of any part of the Members of the League which are cooperating to protect the covenants of the League.

4. Any Member of the League which has violated any covenant of the League may be declared to be no longer a Member of the League by a vote of the Council concurred in by the Representatives of all the other Members of the League represented thereon.

THE NINE POWER TREATY

Concluded at Washington, D. C., February 6, 1922.

The United States of America, Belgium, the British Empire, China, France, Italy, Japan, The Netherlands, and Portugal:

Desiring to adopt a policy designed to stablize conditions in the Far East, to safeguard the rights of interests of China, and to promote intercourse between China and the other powers upon the basis of equality of opportunity;

Article I.—The contracting powers, other than China, agree:

(1) To respect the sovereignty, the independency, and the territorial and administrative integrity of China;

(2) To provide the fullest and most unembarrassed opportunity to China to develop and maintain for herself an effective and stable Government;

(3) To use their influence for the purpose of effectually establishing and maintaining the principle of equal opportunity for the commerce and industry of all nations throughout the territory of China;

(4) To refrain from taking advantage of conditions in China in order to seek special rights or privileges which would abridge the rights of subjects or citizens of friendly States, and from countenancing action inimical to the security of such States;

Article II.—The contracting powers agree not to enter into any treaty, agreement, arrangement or understanding, either with one another, or, individually or collectively, with any power or powers which would infringe or impair the principles stated in Article I.

Article III.—With a view to applying more effectually the principles of the open door or equality of opportunity in China for the trade and industry of all nations, the contracting powers, other than China, agree that they will not seek, nor support their respective nationals in seeking—

(a) Any arrangement which might purport to establish in favor of their interests any general superiority of rights with respect to commercial or economic development in any designated region of China.

(b) Any such monopoly or preference as would deprive the nationals of any other power of the right of undertaking any legitimate trade or industry in China, or of participating with the Chinese Government, or with any local authority in any category of public enterprise, or which by reason of its scope, duration, or geographical extent is calculated to frustrate the practical application of the principle of equal opportunity.

It is understood that the foregoing stipulations of this article are not to be so construed as to prohibit the acquisition of such properties or rights as may be necessary to the conduct of a particular commercial, industrial, or financial undertaking or to the encouragement of invention and research.

China undertakes to be guided by the principles stated in the foregoing stipulations of this article in dealing with applications for economic rights and privileges from Governments and nationals of all foreign countries, whether parties to the present treaty or not.

Article IV.—The contracting powers agree not to support any agreements by their respective nationals with each other designed to create spheres of influence or to provide for the enjoyment of mutually exclusive opportunities in designated parts of Chinese territory.

Article V.—China agrees that, throughout the whole of the railways in China she will not exercise or permit unfair discrimination of any kind. In particular there shall be no discrimination whatever, direct or indirect, in respect of charges or of facilities on the ground of the nationality of passengers or the countries from which or to which they are proceeding, or the origin or ownership of goods or the country from which or to which they are consigned, or the nationality or ownership of the ship or other means of conveying such passengers or goods before or after their transport on the Chinese railways.

The contracting powers, other than China, assume a corresponding obligation in respect of any of the aforesaid railways over which they or their nationals are in a position to exercise any control in virtue of any concession, special agreement or otherwise.

Article VI.—The contracting powers, other than China, agree

fully to respect China's rights as a neutral in time of war to which China is not a party; and China declares that when she is a neutral she will observe the obligations of neutrality.

Article VII.—The contracting powers agree that whenever a situation arises which in the opinion of any one of them involves the application of the stipulations of the present treaty, and renders desirable discussion of such application, there shall be full and frank communication between the contracting powers concerned.

Article VIII.—Powers not signatory to the present treaty, which have governments recognized by the signatory powers and which have treaty relations with China, shall be invited to adhere to the present treaty. To this end the Government of the United States will make the necessary communications to non-signatory powers and will inform the contracting powers of the replies received. Adherence by any power shall become effective on receipt of notice thereof by the Government of the United States.

Article IX.—The present treaty shall be ratified by the contracting powers in accordance with their respective constitutional methods, and shall take effect on the date of the deposit of all the ratifications, which shall take place at Washington as soon as possible. The Government of the United States will transmit to the other contracting powers a certified copy of the process-verbal of the deposit of ratifications.

The present treaty, of which the French and English texts are both authentic, shall remain deposited in the archives of the Government of the United States, and duly certified copies thereof shall be transmitted by that Government to the other contracting powers.

In faith whereof the above-named plenipotentiaries have signed the present treaty.

APPENDIX VII

THE PACT OF PARIS

ARTICLE I

The High Contracting Parties solemnly declare in the names of their respective peoples that they condemn recourse to war for the solution of international controversies, and renounce it as an instrument of national policy in their relations with one another.

Article II

The High Contracting Parties agree that the settlement or solution of all disputes or conflicts of whatever nature or of whatever origin they may be, which may arise among them, shall never be sought expect by pacific means.

Appendix VIII

CASE OF KOREA

BY

Syngman Rhee

President of the Republic of Korea

For more than four thousand years Korea was an independent and sovereign nation. As such, it was recognized and dealt with by all the leading nations of the world.

In various treaties, notably that of alliance against Russia, Feb. 23, 1904, Japan unequivocally guaranteed the independence and territorial integrity of Korea, and the honor and safety of the Korean imperial house. By the terms of this alliance, Japan was permitted to send military forces into and through Korea for the sole purpose of checking the Russian advance, with a solemn pledge that when the war should be over, she would withdraw all·her military forces from Korea. But when the war ended, in direct violation of her agreements, Japan filled the Korean peninsula with her victorious troops, established a protectorate, and in 1910, declared the annexation of Korea, her ally.

Neither the Korean people nor their rulers have ever voluntarily or otherwise surrendered or waived any of Korea's historic rights as an independent and sovereign nation. On the contrary, they have refused to recognize any alleged right or authority of Japan to exercise sovereignty or suzerainty over Korea or any part thereof.

What Has Japan Done to the Korean People Since Annexation?

After the Japanese aggression began in Korea, the Korean Empress was murdered by Japanese soldiers through the conspiracy of the Japanese Minister, her body hacked in pieces, wrapped in tarpaulin, saturated with oil and burned. The Emperor was compelled to abdicate and to live in a secluded palace under guard of Japanese soldiers. In the last days of January 1919, the captive Emperor made an effort to send a delegate to the Peace Conference at Paris to inform the world of Korea's plight and of his incarceration. This was discovered by the Japanese. Almost immediately, it was reported that the Emperor had died of apoplexy. It is believed by all the Koreans that he was poisoned.

The Japanese seized all the Korean telegraph and telephone lines; took control of the postal service; suppressed and confiscated all Korean newspapers; and established a strict censorship—allowing no news of Korea's real condition to be published abroad.

They then seized all Korean public lands, turning them over to Japanese immigrants through the Oriental Development Company. Next they used every conceivable method of coercion to compel the Koreans to give up their holdings. To that end, they ordered the Japanese controlled Bank of Chosen to call in and confiscate all Korean money and specie, thus practically depriving Korea of a circulating medium. They then levied excessive taxes on Korean owned property, which taxes must be paid in money. Having no money, the owners were compelled to give up their homes and lands to the Japanese.

In their efforts to wipe out all the traces of Korean civilization and culture, the Japanese have destroyed Korean historic records and literature, accumulated in more than four thousand years and have attempted to burn all records and documents of the Korean government and people. Laws have been enforced to prohibit the teaching of the Korean language, history and geography in the schools, where as a stroke against Christianity all religious services have been prohibited and Koreans are compelled instead to worship Mikado tablets.

All courts in Korea are presided over by Japanese, and Koreans are unmercifully discriminated against. Korean merchants are not allowed to engage in trade unhampered and Japanese merchants are given distinct advantage over them.

The Japanese regime in Korea in the last twenty years has been an unbroken reign of terror, and individual injuries, wrongs and crimes have been committed and encouraged by Japanese authorities. Korean women have been outraged, wanton murders and massacres have been perpetrated, and an incalculable number of peaceful and unarmed Koreans have been assaulted and robbed by the agents and emissaries of the Government of Japan.

What Are the Evidences That the Korean People Still Want Independence?

The Koreans have never given up the struggle for the restoration of their nation. For that reason, the Japanese Government never dared to withdraw any of its army stations and barracks, the network of which covers the country. Only by these means are the Koreans kept from a nation-wide uprising. The very fact that, in spite of all the subsidies and special advantages offered by their government, the number of Japanese immigrants or colonists in Korea is comparatively insignificant is self-evidence that the Koreans are not kind and friendly enough to make their alien invaders to feel safe and comfortable, and also that Koreans are not "happy and contented under the Mikado's benevolent rule."

After the disbanding of the Korean national forces, the famous Korean "Righteous Armies" or "Irregulars" threatened the existence of the Japanese colonies in the interior. With machine guns the Japanese have combated this menace. But also on pretext of wiping out "bandits" and "insurgents" they have bombarded unfortified towns and villages, massacred innocent men, women and children, and burnt whole villages, to terrorize the entire Korean nation into subjugation.

Despite Japan's elaborate espionage system, the nationalists, by a wonderful system of subterranean correspondence, prepared for a nation-wide uprising. Saturday, March 1, 1919, was chosen as the day to declare their country's independence. Through a network of organizations, copies of the Declaration of Independence were distributed to every local center. A group of 33 nationalist leaders met in secret in Seoul, the Capital of Korea, signed the Declaration, ate a farewell dinner together, telephoned the Japanese police what they had done and sat down to await arrest. One of the signers, having arrived too late for the meeting and dinner, went to the prison and asked to be treated as were the others.

The demonstration broke forth almost simultaneously in three hundred towns and villages, covering every corner of the country.

Thousands of people gathered in public squares, reading the Declaration, shouting "Mansei," (long live Korea), and waving Korean flags. The possession of this flag in Korea was a crime. Women wore it on their dresses. Walls were placarded with it. Men and boys plastered it upon their breasts and offered themselves to the Japanese bayonets. On the opening day and afterwards—until the Japanese drove some of the people to fury—there was no violence.

This, the only wholly peaceful uprising ever recorded of any nation, was suppressed with extreme severity. It is better not to dwell upon the worst phases of the Japanese militarism, as told by independent eye witnesses. The physical manifestations of the movement were crushed, but not the spirit. That smoulders still to flame up again at the first opportunity.

Sentiment of the Korean People in Manchuria

The attitude of the Koreans in Manchuria is correctly expressed in a book "The New Policy for Manchuria and Mongolia," published in Japanese, Nov. 1928, by K. Fujioka, for many years special correspondent for Osaka Mainichi and Tokyo Nichi Nichi in Manchuria and leading newspaper correspondent. He said in part:

"The Koreans, driven by the political and economic forces of the Japanese, have recently migrated to Manchuria, with the hope of recouping there what they had lost at home. The number of the Korean immigrants has rapidly increased recently to more than 3000 each year. This influx was due to the growth of the Chinese nationalistic spirit. The Korean nationalists seek their co-operation and support."

"The Japanese Government should encourage the Korean immigration, because that will help make more room in Korea for Japanese, and at the same time the Koreans cultivate the waste land of Manchuria for the ultimate benefit of the Japanese. But instead of encouraging it, the Government is favoring the Korean persecution policy and tries to keep the Koreans from being naturalized as Chinese citizens, which is decidedly a mistaken policy. . . ."

These quotations clearly show that the Japanese Government, realizing the danger of Chinese-Korean co-operation, has been instigating on the one hand, persecution and intrigues against the Koreans, while on the other, openly encroaching upon the sovereign rights of China by extending police and military jurisdiction over Chinese territory wherever the Koreans are found. For this the excuse is given that the Koreans are the Mikado's subjects and need protection. Of course, the Koreans resented this assertion but were not in a position to declare publicly their feelings. The Chinese on the other hand, facing the difficulties of a dual citizenship in their land, would not welcome the Koreans. But the friendly feelings existing so many centuries between Koreans and Chinese still hold strong. The Chinese understanding the motives behind the intrigues and persecutions sympathize with Koreans.

When the Independence Demonstrations were taking place in 1919, Koreans in Manchuria and Siberia, like all Koreans everywhere, held mass meetings in which they read the Declaration of Independence, waved their flags and shouted "Mansei." At Yong Jung in Chientao, the Chinese hirelings of the Japanese Consulate fired at the crowds, which were dispersing in perfect order after the celebration. Seventeen Koreans were killed. The Government of Kirin, being under the influence of Japanese, no redress was obtained.

In Oct. 1920, against the strongest protest from China, Japan sent 15,000 soldiers into Chientao pretending that their mission was "to clean up the bandits." Dr. H. S. Martin, a Canadian Presbyterian missionary to Yong Jung, an impartial witness, testified that "the Japanese methodically burned village after village, shooting the young men in each, so that" says Dr. Martin, "at present we have a ring of villages surrounding this city that have suffered from fire or murder or both."

I have neither the desire nor the space to quote any of the most horrifying stories of the Japanese atrocities committed on the Koreans in this one aggression. Suffice it to say that the corroboration of the figures compiled by the Chinese and British in that district show:

Inhabitants murdered 3128
Arrests 238
Women assaulted 76
Houses burned 2404
Schools destroyed 31
Churches burned 10
Grain burned .... 40,931 suk
(approximately 818,620 bushels)

Since Sept. 18, 1931, many Koreans have been massacred in various parts of Manchuria, by the Chinese, instigated by the Japanese. The news dispatches from Japanese sources reported these massacres to create an impression that the Koreans ask the Japanese soldiers to protect them. But in truth, more Koreans were massacred by the Japanese themselves than by the Chinese mercenaries.

The Koreans in Manchuria, as the Koreans everywhere else, believe that Japan is wholly unfit to dominate their country. They deny the validity of Japan's pretentions to a superior civilization. They denounce its aggressions as international Banditry and they assert the indestructible right of Korea to its own existence and its own freedom.

APPENDIX IX

SUMMARY OF THE REPORTS OF THE LEAGUE OF NATIONS MEETINGS

Based on the League of Nations' Official Journal.

Sept. 21, 1931. China invokes Article II of the League of Nations Covenant to "bring to the attention of the Assembly or of the Council any circumstances whatever affecting international relations which threaten to disturb international peace or good understanding between nations upon which peace depends."

Sept. 22, 1931. China agrees to League inquiry but demands that *status quo ante* be restored.

Japan insists on direct negotiation.

The Council unanimously decided to request China and Japan (1) to adopt a peaceful means of settlement; (2) to immediately proceed to withdraw their troops; and (3) to forward to the United States the minutes of its meetings.

Sept. 23, 1931. Japan disapproves of the appointment of an international commission.

Sept. 24, 1931. The United States approves of the League of Nations resolution.

Japan accepts the same resolution.

Sept. 25, 1931. Japan accepts the League resolution of Sept. 22.

Sept. 28, 1931. China compromises with Japan's objection to inquiry by neutral commission and suggests that the League facilitate settlement on the spot by appointing neutrals on the spot to represent the League and to supervise withdrawal of Japanese troops.
Japan still refuses outside observers.

Sept. 30, 1931. League Council adopts resolution summarized as follows:

1. The League Council notes replies from China and Japan.

2. Recognized that Japan has no territorial designs.

3. Notes that Japan will withdraw her troops as rapidly as possible.

4. China will assume responsibility for Japanese life and property.

5. Notes both have given assurances not to extend the incident nor to aggravate the situation.

6. Requests both to rapidly execute the above.

7. Requests both to keep the Council informed.

8. Decides to reconvene October 14.

9. Authorizes President to cancel Oct. 14 meeting if situation no longer requires it.

Oct. 8, 1931. Japan bombs Chinchow.
China requests immediate reconvening of the League Council.

Oct. 12, 1931. Japan demands that China agree upon certain fundamental principles before her troops be withdrawn from Chinese territory.
The United States reaffirms its intention of cooperating with the League.

Oct. 13, 1931. The League Council meets.
China states that Japanese troops must be withdrawn from Chinese territory before discussion.

Oct. 15, 1931. The United States signifies its willingness to appoint a representative if invited to sit with Council.
Japan alone refuses to agree to invite the United States.

Oct. 16, 1931. The League Council invites the United States to its meetings.
Japan objects and casts the only dissenting vote.

Oct. 17, 1931. The Pact of Paris (Briand-Kellogg Pact) is invoked.

Oct. 21, 1931. Japan presents five points:
(1) Both China and Japan not to commit acts of aggression.
(2) Both refrain from hostile agitation, boycotts and propaganda.
(3) Japan to respect the territorial integrity of Manchuria.
(4) China to guarantee protection of Japanese subjects in Manchuria.
(5) China and Japan to provide for cooperation in avoiding ruinous railway competition and China to give effect to all existing railway treaties.

China presents four points:
(1) No negotiations before the withdrawal of Japanese troops.
(2) Neutral investigation during and after withdrawal.
(3) China and Japan to negotiate on the question of reparations for damages done by Japanese troops.
(4) A permanent Board of Conciliation to settle all outstanding disputes.

Oct. 22, 1931. Briand presents draft of resolution.
(1) The League Council requests the pledge of Japan to withdraw her troops as soon as possible, and of China to protect Japanese life and property.
(2) Council requests pledges of both parties not to aggravate the situation.
(3) Council requests Japan's statement that Japan has no territorial designs in Manchuria.

(4) (a) Calls upon Japan to immediately begin troop withdrawal and complete withdrawal by November 16, 1931; (b) Calls upon China to arrange for security of life and property in area to be evacuated.

(5) Recommends that both should immediately appoint representatives to work out details of above arrangement.

(6) Recommends that as soon as evacuation is completed, both begin direct negotiations on outstanding questions. For this purpose the Council suggests a permanent Conciliation Commission be set up.

(7) Council decides to adjourn until November 16, 1931, but authorizes the President to convoke early meeting if necessary.

Oct. 23, 1931. China willing to accept and offers assistance to foreigners in providing security.

Japan objects to resolution and offers counter-resolution that Japan will not withdraw until China and Japan settle certain fundamental principles.

Oct. 24, 1931. Council attempts to make Japan specifically define the fundamental principles referred to, and she refuses.

Japan's counter-resolution put to a vote and was defeated 13 to 1.

Council passes its resolution "unanimously minus one vote."

China offers to submit treaty interpretations to judicial settlement as in Article 13 of the Covenant.

Nov. 6, 1931. United States notifies Tokio that it has associated itself with League resolution.

Nov. 12, 1931. United States orders Dawes to Paris for Council meeting.

Nov. 16, 1931. Council meets in Paris.

Nov. 17, 1931. Nine Power Treaty brought into discussion.

Nov. 18, 1931. Japan occupies Tsitsihar.

Nov. 19, 1931. Council turns to September proposal for international inquiry.

Nov. 21, 1931. Japan agrees to inquiry with reservations that it should not interfere with direct negotiations nor supervise military movements.

Nov. 25, 1931. League warns China and Japan against further hostilities.

League presses China for acceptance of inquiry.

League considers a plan for neutralizing Chinchow area. China welcomes.

Nov. 27-28, 1931. Japan indignant against Stimson for reported remarks.

Nov. 29, 1931. Japan objects to neutralizing Chinchow area.

Nov. 30, 1931. China willing to drop demand of fixed date for Japan's withdrawal if proposed inquiry is allowed to report on matter.

Japan wants drafted resolution modified in regard to early evacuation.

Dec. 1, 1931. Council present revised draft to China and Japan.

Dec. 2, 1931. Japan approves Chinchow neutral zone if (a) Chinese troops withdraw and (b) policing of zone left to Japan and local Chinese.

Dec. 5, 1931. China refuses to evacuate Chinchow under Japan's conditions.

Japan puts up two more obstacles to drafting of resolution: (1) the inquiry should not interfere with army and (2) Japan must police an indefinite area against banditry.

Dec. 7, 1931. Japan wants neutral zone to exclude Chinchow. China again refuses to evacuate under Japan's conditions.

League makes public its proposed resolutions:

(1) Calls upon China and Japan to execute resolution of September 30.

(2) Notes that both will refrain from further aggravating activities.

(3) Invites both to keep League informed.

(4) Decides to appoint Commission of five to study on the spot and "to report to the Council on any circumstances which, affecting international relations, threaten to disturb peace between China and Japan or the good understanding on which peace depends."

(5) Japan and China each may appoint one assessor to assist Commission. Both countries to facilitate its work.

(6) Commission not to interfere with direct negotiation or military movements.

(7) Japan is still expected to withdraw troops as agreed in September 30 resolution.

(8) President is charged to follow up question between adjournment and next session of January 25.

Dec. 10, 1931. Resolution passed unanimously.

Japan makes reservation that resolution does not prejudice the right of Japan to protect Japanese life and property against bandits and lawless elements.

China makes 8 reservations.

Latin American states make 4 reservations.

United States approves resolution.

Jan. 25, 1932. Council convened at Geneva.

Jan. 28, 1932. China and Japan agree to defray the expenses of the Commission set up in virtue of the Resolution of Dec. 10, 1931.

Jan. 29, 1932. Shanghai attacked by Japanese forces.

China invokes Articles X and XV of the Covenant.

Jan. 30, 1932. Japan disagrees with other members of the Council that Article 15 is applicable to the dispute.

Feb. 2, 1932. Council appoints Committee in Shanghai to observe and report events on the spot.

Feb. 9, 1932. Discusses procedure to act under Article XV.

Feb. 19, 1932. Passes resolution to refer the dispute to the Assembly in accordance with Article XV over the objections of Japan.

March 3, 1932. Extraordinary session of the Assembly.

March 4, 1932. Assembly passes the following resolutions:

(1) Asks both China and Japan to cease hostilities.

(2) Requests representatives of neutral powers at Shanghai to keep Assembly informed about the execution of (1).

(3) Recommends that the same representatives regulate the withdrawal of Japanese forces.

March 11, 1932. Assembly representing 46 nations adopts a resolution which is summarized as follows:

(1) It is incumbent upon members of the League of Nations not to recognize any situation, treatment, or agreement, brought about by means contrary to the Covenant.

(2) Reaffirm the Assembly's March 4 resolution.

(3) Refers the whole Sino-Japanese dispute to a Committee of Nineteen members to act in behalf of the Assembly.

APPENDIX X

REFERENCES (*Partial List*)

1. Willoughby, W. W.   Foreign Rights and Interests in China (Revised Edition). 2 Vols.
2. Hornbeck, Stanley K.   Contemporary Politics in the Far East.
3. Hsii, Shuhsi.   China and Her Political Entity.
4. Young, C. Walter.   Japan's Special Position in Manchuria.
5. Reinsch, Paul S.   An American Diplomat in China.

6. Clark, Grover. Manchuria: A Survey of Its Economic Development.

7. Bain, H. Foster. Ores and Industry in the Far East.

8. Hosie, Alexander. Manchuria, Its People, Resources, and Recent History.

9. Field, Frederick V. American Participation in the China Consortiums.

10. Hobicht, Max. Post-War Treaties for the Pacific Settlement of International Disputes.

11. League of Nations. Official Journal.

—— Verbatim Report of the Extraordinary Session of the Assembly.